XENIX Commands and DOS Cross Development Services:

Programmer's Rapid Reference

XENIX Commands and DOS Cross Development Services:

Programmer's Rapid Reference

Baird Peterson, Ph.D.

VAN NOSTRAND REINHOLD
New York

Copyright © 1992 by Van Nostrand Reinhold

Library of Congress Catalog Card Number 91-19949
ISBN 0-442-00540-7

Manufactured in the United States of America

Published by Van Nostrand Reinhold
115 Fifth Avenue
New York, New York 10003

Chapman and Hall
2-6 Boundary Row
London, SE1 8HN, England

Thomas Nelson Australia
102 Dodds Street
South Melbourne 3205
Victoria, Australia

Nelson Canada
1120 Birchmount Road
Scarborough, Ontario M1K 5G4, Canada

16 15 14 13 12 11 10 9 8 7 6 5 4 3 2 1

Library of Congress Cataloging-in-Publication Data
Peterson, Baird.
    XENIX commands and DOS cross development services : programmer's
rapid reference / Baird Peterson.
        p.   cm.
    Includes bibliographical references (p.   ) and index.
    ISBN 0-442-00540-7
    1. Operating systems (Computers) 2. XENIX   I. Title.
QA76.76.063P527   1992   91-19949
005.4'46--dc20   CIP

to Maureen,
Colin,
and my mother

Contents

Preface   xi

Acknowledgments   xiii

Introduction   1
    How to Use This Book   2

Part 1. XENIX Commands   3
    intro (CP) PROGRAMMING COMMANDS intro (CP)   3
    class (CP) COMMAND CLASSIFICATION class (CP)   5
    adb (CP) DEBUGGING AIDS adb (CP)   7
    admin (CP) SOURCE CODE CONTROL SYSTEM admin (CP)   16
    ar (CP) LIBRARY MANAGEMENT ar (CP)   20
    asx (CP) ASSEMBLY/DISASSEMBLY asx (CP)   22
    cb (CP) DEBUGGING AIDS cb (CP)   23
    cc (CP) C COMPILATION cc (CP)   24
    cdc (CP) SOURCE CODE CONTROL SYSTEM cdc (CP)   32
    cflow (CP) C DEBUGGING AIDS cflow (CP)   34
    comb (CP) SOURCE CODE CONTROL SYSTEM comb (CP)   36
    cpp (CP) C PREPROCESSOR cpp (CP)   37
    cref (CP) DEBUGGING AIDS cref (CP)   40

ctags (CP) DEBUGGING AIDS ctags (CP)   41
cxref (CP) DEBUGGING AIDS cxref (CP)   42
delta (CP) SOURCE CODE CONTROL SYSTEM delta (CP)   43
dosld (CP) CROSS DEVELOPMENT UTILITY dosld (CP)   46
get (CP) SOURCE CODE CONTROL SYSTEM get (CP)   47
gets (CP) STRING INPUT gets (CP)   53
hdr (CP) XENIX COMPATIBILITY hdr (CP)   53
help (CP) SOURCE CODE CONTROL SYSTEM help (CP)   55
ld (CP) LINK EDITING ld (CP)   56
lex (CP) LEXICAL/SYNTACTICAL ANALYSIS lex (CP)   58
lint (CP) DEBUGGING AIDS lint (CP)   61
lorder (CP) LIBRARY MANAGEMENT lorder (CP)   64
m4 (CP) PREPROCESSOR m4 (CP)   65
make (CP) VERSION CONTROL make (CP)   69
masm (CP) SOFTWARE DEVELOPMENT COMMANDS   77
mkstr (CP) C STRING MANIPULATION mkstr (CP)   79
nm (CP) OBJECT FILE MANIPULATION nm (CP)   81
prof (CP) PROFILING prof (CP)   82
prs (CP) SOURCE CODE CONTROL SYSTEM prs (CP)   84
ranlib (CP) LIBRARY MANAGEMENT ranlib (CP)   87
ratfor (CP) CONVERT RATFOR TO FORTRAN ratfor (CP)   88
regcmp (CP) C COMPILATION regcmp (CP)   90
rmdel (CP) SOURCE CODE CONTROL SYSTEM rmdel (CP)   90
sact (CP) SOURCE CODE CONTROL SYSTEM sact (CP)   92
sccsdiff (CP) SOURCE CODE CONTROL SYSTEM   93
sdb (CP) DEBUGGING sdb (CP)   94
size (CP) OBJECT FILE MANIPULATION size (CP)   101
spline MATHEMATICAL UTILITY spline (CP)   102
strings (CP) OBJECT FILE MANIPULATION strings (CP)   103
strip (CP) OBJECT FILE MANIPULATION strip (CP)   104
tic (CP) TERMINAL INFORMATION tic (CP)   105
time (CP) PROFILING time (CP)   106
tsort (CP) SORTING tsort (CP)   107
unget (CP) SOURCE CODE CONTROL SYSTEM unget (CP)   107
val (CP) SOURCE CODE CONTROL SYSTEM val (CP)   108
what (CP) SOURCE CODE CONTROL SYSTEM what (CP)   110
xref (CP) DEBUGGING AIDS xref (CP)   111
xstr (CP) C STRING MANIPULATION xstr (CP)   112
yacc (CP) LEXICAL/SYNTACTIC ANALYSIS yacc (CP)   114

Part 2. DOS Cross Development Services   117
intro (DOS) DOS CROSS DEVELOPMENT intro (DOS)   117
class (DOS) SYSTEM CALL CLASSIFICATION class (DOS)   118

bdos (DOS) DOS SYSTEM CALLS bdos (DOS)   121
cgets (DOS) CONSOLE INPUT cgets (DOS)   122
cprintf (DOS) CONSOLE OUTPUT cprintf (DOS)   123
cputs (DOS) CONSOLE OUTPUT cputs (DOS)   126
cscanf (DOS) CONSOLE INPUT cscanf (DOS)   126
dosexterr (DOS) DOS SYSTEM CALLS dosexterr (DOS)   129
eof (DOS) FILE OPERATIONS eof (DOS)   130
exit (DOS) PROCESS CONTROL exit (DOS)   131
fclose (DOS) STREAMS OPERATIONS fclose (DOS)   132
fcloseall (DOS) STREAMS OPERATIONS fcloseall (DOS)   132
fgetc (DOS) STREAM INPUT fgetc (DOS)   133
fgetchar (DOS) STREAM INPUT fgetchar (DOS)   133
filelength (DOS) FILE OPERATIONS filelength (DOS)   134
flushall (DOS) BUFFER OUTPUT flushall (DOS)   135
FP__OFF (DOS) GET ADDRESS REGISTERS FP__OFF (DOS)   136
FP__SEG (DOS) GET ADDRESS REGISTERS FP__SEG (DOS)   136
fputc (DOS) STREAM OUTPUT fputc (DOS)   137
fputchar (DOS) STREAM OUTPUT fputchar (DOS)   137
getch (DOS) CONSOLE INPUT getch (DOS)   138
getche (DOS) CONSOLE INPUT getche (DOS)   139
inp (DOS) CONSOLE INPUT inp (DOS)   140
int86 (DOS) SOFTWARE INTERRUPTS int86 (DOS)   140
int86x (DOS) DOS SYSTEM CALLS int86x (DOS)   141
intdos (DOS) DOS SYSTEM CALLS intdos (DOS)   143
intdosx (DOS) DOS SYSTEM CALLS intdosx (DOS)   144
isatty (DOS) FILE OPERATIONS isatty (DOS)   145
itoa (DOS) VARIABLE CONVERSION itoa (DOS)   146
kbhit (DOS) CONSOLE INPUT kbhit (DOS)   147
labs (DOS) INTEGER OPERATIONS labs (DOS)   148
ltoa (DOS) VARIABLE CONVERSIONS ltoa (DOS)   149
mkdir (DOS) DIRECTORY OPERATIONS mkdir (DOS)   150
movedata (DOS) MOVE BYTES IN MEMORY movedata (DOS)   150
outp (DOS) PORT OUTPUT outp (DOS)   152
putch (DOS) CONSOLE OUTPUT putch (DOS)   153
rename (DOS) DIRECTORY OPERATIONS rename (DOS)   153
rmdir (DOS) DIRECTORY OPERATIONS rmdir (DOS)   154
segread (DOS) GET ADDRESS REGISTERS segread (DOS)   155
setmode (DOS) FILE OPERATIONS setmode (DOS)   156
sopen (DOS) FILE OPERATIONS sopen (DOS)   157
spawnl (DOS) PROCESS CONTROL spawnl (DOS)   160
spawnvp (DOS) PROCESS CONTROL spawnvp (DOS)   160
strlen (DOS) STRING OPERATIONS strlen (DOS)   165
strlwr (DOS) STRING OPERATIONS strlwr (DOS)   166

strrev (DOS) STRING OPERATIONS strrev (DOS)   167
strset (DOS) STRING OPERATIONS strset (DOS)   167
strupr (DOS) STRING OPERATIONS strupr (DOS)   168
tell (DOS) FILE OPERATIONS tell (DOS)   169
ultoa (DOS) VARIABLE CONVERSIONS ultoa (DOS)   170
ungetch (DOS) CONSOLE OUTPUT ungetch (DOS)   171

Bibliography   173

Index   177

Preface

XENIX Commands and DOS Cross Development Services: Programmer's Rapid Reference was written to help several different kinds of readers. It covers material that UNIX programmers need to know in order to port software applications from UNIX to XENIX. With more than 400,000 units of XENIX sold and with as many as 3 million XENIX users, XENIX is the most common variety of UNIX. For years to come, UNIX programmers will be porting UNIX software to XENIX in order to take advantage of an installed XENIX base that is still adding thousands of new users each year.

This book also covers material that XENIX programmers need to know in order to port a XENIX application to UNIX, since it gives all of the details about XENIX software development commands and system services for which the programmer must find UNIX counterparts.

In addition, this book supports students and others who choose to do software development work using an inexpensive UNIX development system—XENIX.

XENIX Commands and DOS Cross Services: Programmer's Rapid Reference has features that help newcomers find descriptions of XENIX software development commands and DOS cross development services quickly, without having to know the names of any of these commands or services. Also the descriptions of Xenix features are organized to reduce research time, something that every reader will enjoy.

XENIX has hundreds of commands, system services, library routines, and file formats. This book describes all SCO XENIX commands that are used in general software development. It also describes all of the SCO XENIX system services used for cross development of DOS software. This book, together with *XENIX System V System Services: Programmer's Rapid Reference,* by Baird Peterson, describes all of the XENIX commands and system services normally needed for XENIX software development. See SCO XENIX documentation for descriptions of other XENIX commands used by system administrators and users.

cc, the C compiler supplied with XENIX, can generate code for the 8086, 80186, 80286 (XENIX 286), or 80386 (XENIX 386), depending on the compiler options selected. This book describes all options of cc and indicates which XENIX commands and options pertain to 8086, 80186, 80286, or 80386 chips.

Acknowledgments

Many people helped to create this book. I thank my literary agent, Bill Gladstone of Waterside Productions, Inc. I also thank the people at Van Nostrand Reinhold, especially Dianne Littwin, acquisition editor; Alberta Gordon, managing editor; Paul Sobel, developmental editor; and Robert Gasperi, editorial assistant. I thank my anonymous reviewers for helping to make this a better book. I thank Adele Just for her excellent editorial help. I thank my wife Maureen for her constant support and encouragement.

XENIX Commands and DOS Cross Development Services: Programmer's Rapid Reference

Introduction

Notation

The following kinds of notation are used in this book.

`constant width italic type` denotes the names of variables to which specific values must be assigned.

`constant width roman type` denotes input such as commands and options.

`command` ([*name year*[*letter*]|*letter*]) refers to a book or to a section of this book where a description of the specified `command` may be found. The form

<code>command</code> (letter)

refers to a description in Part 1 of this book, `command` (CP), or to a description in Part 2, `systemcall` (DOS). The form

<code>command</code> (name year[letter])

gives the author *name* of a book listed in the bibliograpy of this book, the *year* the listed book was published, and the specific book (*letter*) published in that *year* if the author had more than one book published in that year. For example,

<code>csh</code> (SCO 1988j)

refers to a description of `csh` in one of several books written by the Santa Cruz Operation in 1988.

`<>` indicates input that is not displayed on the screen when it is typed, for example, passwords, tabs, or RETURN. Such input appears between angle brackets. The angle brackets themselves are not input.

`<^char>` indicates control characters. The circumflex (ˆ) denotes the control key (CTRL), while `char` denotes some key. For example, `<^d>` denotes

1

the value obtained by holding the control key down and striking the D key. The letter *D* is not displayed, and the angle brackets themselves are not input. [] indicates optional arguments and command options. One or more of the options enclosed by the square brackets (but not the brackets themselves) are input. | separates optional arguments in cases where only one of two listed options may be chosen. For example, in the following command:

$$command\ [arg1|arg2]$$

either *arg1* or *arg2* may be chosen, but not both
.... means that more than one argument like the preceding argument may be used on a command line.

How to Use This Book

If you are an experienced XENIX programmer and you already know all the names of XENIX commands, see Part 1 for the description of a command, or see Part 2 for the description of a system call for DOS cross development. The descriptive entries are given in alphabetical order.

If you are a newcomer to XENIX programming, read the following two sections.

Classification of Commands and System Calls

If you don't know the names of all of the XENIX commands and system calls used for software development, turn to page 5 to read the section that classifies XENIX commands. Then turn to page 118 to read the section that classifies DOS cross development services.

Useful XENIX Commands

XENIX offers quite a few commands that a newcomer can use to learn about the XENIX system.

[help] glossary [*term*] gives definitions of common XENIX technical terms and symbols.

[help] provides on-line help information for XENIX users.

[help] locate gives on-line help in identifying appropriate XENIX system commands.

[help] starter provides several categories of XENIX system information.

[help] usage gives examples of the usage of commands.

Part I

XENIX Commands

This chapter consists of three main parts:

- An explanation of the format of the entries that describe XENIX commands,
- A command classification table (page 5) that helps you quickly find the appropriate command call for your purpose, and
- The descriptive entries themselves in alphabetical order.

Format of Command Descriptions

Each descriptive entry consists of up to seven separate sections: Name, Synopsis, Description, Options and Arguments, Files, See Also, and Warning Notes.

Name

The name of each command is followed by a brief phrase describing its purpose.

Synopsis

The synopsis shows a command and any options and arguments that it accepts according to the following syntax:

$$command\ [option(\text{s})]\ [commandarg(\text{s})]$$

where:

> *command* specifies an executable file,
> *option* is either − *argletternoopt*(s) or − *argletter op-*
tionarg

where

> *argletternoopt*, a single letter, represents an option that requires no option argument,
> *argletter*, a single letter, represents an option that requires an option argument, followed by optional spaces, and
> *optionarg* is a character string specifying an argument for the previous *argletter*.
> *commandarg*(s) is "−" by itself, indicating standard input, or is a pathname or other command argument that does not begin with "−".

Description
Each description contains general details about the system call.

Options and Arguments
Where possible (and it nearly always is), all of the information about each argument of a command is put in this subsection. The descriptions of arguments are sorted in ASCII order of the argument names as these are given in the synopsis, except that when an argument is preceded by a " + " it is grouped with other arguments that are preceded by "−". Usually, when information about an argument must appear in other subsections, or in the material about another argument, the argument description will point to such material.

Files
In general, this section describes various files and directories used by the command. Several descriptive entries refer to *BINDIR*, *INCDIR*, *LIBDIR*, *LLIBDIR*, and *TMPDIR*. These five names represent directory names whose actual values are specified where necessary.

See Also
This section points to related commands.

Warning Notes
Normally, any warnings associated with the use of a particular option or argument are given in the description for that option or argument. This section contains more general notes and warnings.

class (CP)   **COMMAND CLASSIFICATION**   **class (CP)**

This section classifies the 49 commands described in this chapter.

C Programming Utilities

Compilation
    cc—C compiler   24
    regcmp—compile a regular expression   90

C String Manipulation
    mkstr—create an error message file from a C source   79
    xstr—extract strings from C programs   112

Debugging Aids
    cb—C program beautifier   23
    cflow—make a C flowgraph charting external references   34
    ctags—create a tags file for *vi* from C sources   41
    cxref—create a cross-reference table for a C program   42
    lint—check C programs for bad features   61
    xref—cross-reference C programs   111

Preprocessor
    cpp—C language preprocessor invoked by the cc command   37

Cross-Development Utilities
    dosld—MS-DOS cross-linker   46

Mathematical Utilities
    spline—interpolates a smooth curve   102

Software Generation Utilities for Various Languages
Assembly/Disassembly
    asx—XENIX 8086/186/286 assembler   22
    masm—invoke an assembler   77

Convert RATFOR S/W to FORTRAN S/W
    ratfor—converts Rational FORTRAN to standard FORTRAN   88

Debugging
    adb—invoke a general-purpose debugger   7
    cref—make cross-reference listing (assembler or C)   40
    sdb—call a symbolic debugger   94

Lexical/Syntactic Analysis
   lex—generate programs to do lexical analysis of text   58
   yacc—yet another compiler-compiler   114

Library Management
   ar—maintain archive files   20
   lorder—get an ordering relation for an object library   64
   ranlib—convert archives to random libraries   87

Link Editing
   ld—link-edit common object files   56

Object File Manipulation
   nm—display a symbol table of common object file(s)   81
   size—print a section size of common object files   101
   strings—look for ASCII strings in an object file   103
   strip—strip symbol table and line numbers from file(s)   104

Preprocessor
   m4—macroprocessor for various languages   65

Profiling
   prof—display profile data produced by *monitor* function   82
   time—times execution of a command   106

Sorting
   tsort—topological sort   107

Version Control
   make—maintain, update, or regenerate groups of programs   69

Source Code Control System
   admin—create SCCS files or alter SCCS file parameters   16
   cdc—change delta commentary in SCCS s-file(s)   32
   comb—generate shell procedure to reconstruct SCCS files   36
   delta—make a change (delta) to an SCCS file   43
   get—generate ASCII text from an SCCS file   47
   help—get help about SCCS commands   55
   prs—print an SCCS file   84
   rmdel—remove a delta (change) from an SCCS file   90
   sact—announce any impending deltas to an SCCS file   92
   sccsdiff—compare versions of an SCCS file   93

unget—undo a prior *get* of an SCCS file   107
val—validate an SCCS file   108
what—identify SCCS file by searching for a pattern   110

String Input
gets—gets a string from *stdin*   53

Terminal Information Utilities
tic—compile a *terminfo* file   105

XENIX Compatibility Utilities
hdr—display parts of a XENIX object file   53

adb (CP)	DEBUGGING	adb (CP)

Name

adb—invoke a general-purpose debugger

Synopsis

adb [-w] [-p *prompt*] [*objfile*] [*corefile*]
or
adb *outfile*

Description

The adb program is a general-purpose debugger that provides a controlled environment for executing XENIX programs. It may be used to examine files even if the files lack symbol tables, although other features of adb cannot be used in such a case. COFF or x.out files can be read transparently.

The adb program reads requests from the standard input and sends its responses to the standard output. After adb presents a prompt, the user may make requests to adb that have the following form:

[*address*] [,*count*] [*command*] [;]

where

• *address* is a value or expression that gives the location of the instruction or data item, causing the current file position (*dot*) to be set to the value specified by address. *dot* initially is set to zero;

- *count* specifies the number of times the *command* is to be executed (default is 1), and
- *command* is one of the commands shown in the following section.

address is a special expression with the following form:

$$[segment:]offset$$

where *segment* specifies the address of a text or data segment and *offset* specifies the offset from the beginning of that segment. The last segment value specified in a command is used if *segment* is not given in the current adb request.

Commands

Most adb commands have a verb followed by either a modifier or a list of modifiers. The available commands are as follows.

Dot Operations
See the $r command and *dot* (Current Address) under "Outputting Information."
Assign Dot to Register or Variable
>*name* assigns *dot* to the named register or variable.
Make Dot Permanent
newline makes a temporary *dot* increment permanent if the previous command temporarily incremented *dot*. Repeat the previous command with *count* equal to 1.

Exiting adb
The $q command will stop adb and cause a return to the shell. Also, the <CTRL>D command will stop adb. Neither the Quit nor the Interrupt key will stop adb. The adb command catches Interrupt and waits for a new command. It ignores Quit entirely.

Finding (Matching) Words
[?/]l *value mask* or [?/]L *value mask* uses *mask* to mask words starting at *dot* and to compare the words with *value* until it finds a match. If L is used in stead of l, the match is for 4 bytes at once instead of 2 bytes. *dot* is unchanged if no match is found; otherwise, *dot* is the address of the location where the match occurred. The default value of *mask* is −1.
$s sets the limit for symbol matches to *address* instead of the default, 255.

Formatting
See the $v command under "Outputting Information."

$d sets the default I/O format to decimal.
$o sets the default I/O format to octal.
$v prints all nonzero variables in octal. See "Octal Variables" under "Outputting Information."
$w sets the page width for output to *address* (default is 80).
$x sets the default I/O format to hexadecimal.

Inputting
! calls a shell to read the remainder of the line following '!'.
$<*file* reads commands from *file* and returns.

Memory Segment Creation or Modification
[?/]m *segnum filpos size* assigns new size and file position values to a specified segment. The segment number, *segnum*, must be that of a segment already in the memory map. Only the file position is changed if *size* is omitted. If / is used in the command, the segment altered is a data segment. Otherwise, if ? is used, the segment is a text segment.
[?/]M *segnum filpos size* creates a segment in the memory map with file position *filpos* and segment size *size*. The segment number, *segnum*, must not already exist in the memory map. If / is used in the command, the segment created is a data segment. Otherwise, if ? is used, the segment is a text segment.

Outputting Information
$*modifier* is the form of several commands used to print the contents of various registers or other variables. The values of *modifier* are as follows:
$b prints every breakpoint, and the count and command associated with it.
$c performs a C stack backtrace. If *count* is specified, only the first *count* frames are printed. If *address* is specified, *address* is used as the address of the current frame instead of bp.
$e prints the names and values of external variables.
$f prints the floating registers in single or double length.
$>*file* sends output to the file, *file*, creating *file* if it does not exist.
$m prints the address map.
$r prints the general registers and the instruction to which ip points. It also sets *dot* to ip.
$v prints all nonzero variables in octal.
The following three commands print out address values or contents:

? *f* prints the contents of locations in *objfile*, starting at text *address*, according to format *f*.

/ *f* prints the contents of locations in *corefile*, starting at data *address*, according to format *f*.

= *f* prints the value of *address* in the style specified by *f*. If the format is **i**, "?" is printed for those parts of the instruction that refer to subsequent words.

The format, *f*, is one or more characters that specify the printing format. A decimal integer repeat count may precede each format character. While a format specification is being stepped through, *dot* (current address) is temporarily incremented by the amount specified for each format letter. The last format character used is used again if no format character is specified.

The format letters available, and the values printed, are as follows:

Character and String Variables

    c is a 1-byte character (type char variables)

    C is an an addressed character, escaped as follows:

character values from 000 to 040 are printed as an at-sign (@) followed by the corresponding character in the range 0100 to 0140 (octal). The at-sign is printed as @@.

    s ia a null-terminated character string.

    S prints a string using the at-sign (@) escape convention as in C above.

    "..." prints the quote-enclosed string.

Date

    Y is 4 bytes in the date format shown in *ctime* (Peterson 1992).

Decimal Variables

    d is a 2-byte decimal (type int variable).

    D is a 4-byte decimal (type long variable).

    u is a 2-byte unsigned decimal (type int variable).

    U is a 4-byte unsigned decimal (type long variable).

Dot (Current Address)

    See the **$r** command under "Outputting Information."

    ^ decrements *dot* by the current increment; it prints nothing.

    + increments *dot* by 1; it prints nothing.

    − decrements *dot* by 1; it prints nothing.

    a prints *dot* value in symbolic form after testing symbols to ensure that they are

- local or global data symbols if the command is **/** *f*,
- local or global text symbols if the command is **/** *f*, or
- local or absolute symbols if the command is **=** *f*.

    A prints the *dot* value in absolute form.

Floating Point

 f prints 4-byte single-precision floating point.

 F prints 8-byte double-precision floating point.

Hexadecimal Variables

 x prints 2-byte hexadecimal (type int variable).

 X prints 4-byte hexadecimal (type long variable).

Machine Instruction

 i prints the machine instruction. Variables 1 and 2 are set to the offset parts of the source and destination, respectively.

Octal Variables

 Any octal number printed by *adb* is preceded by 0.

 b prints the individual addressed byte in octal.

 o prints 2-byte octal (type int variable).

 O prints 4-byte octal.

 q prints signed octal.

 Q prints long signed octal.

Spaces, Tabs, and Newlines

 p prints the addressed value in symbolic form. It uses the same symbol table lookup rules describe for a above.

 t tabs to the next appropriate tab stop when t is preceded by an integer.

 r prints a spece.

 n prints a newline.

Subprocess Management

 :*modifier* is the form of commands for managing a subprocess. The modifiers are as follows:

Continue Execution After Breakpoint Stop

 co*s* continues the subprocess and passes signal *s* to it. The signal that made the subprocess stop is sent if no signal is specified. Breakpoint skipping operates the same way as with r below. The subprocess is continued at *address* if *address* is specified.

 s*s* has the same action as co above, except that the subprocess is single-stepped *count* times. If no current subprocess exists, *objfile* is executed as a subprocess, the same way as in r above. No signal can be sent in this case, and the remainder of the command line is used as arguments to the subprocess.

Delete Breakpoint

 d1 deletes the breakpoint at *address*.

Execute Program

 r[*arguments*] executes *objfile* as a subprocess. Execution begins at the standard entry point of *objfile* unless *address* is explicitly specified, in which case entry is at *address*. On entry to the subprocess, all signals are turned on. *count* tells how many breakpoints are to be ignored before stopping. The subprocess may have *arguments* specified on the command line following *r*. Any argument that starts with < or > establishes the standard input or standard output as input or output for the command.

R[*arguments*] has the same action as *r* above, except that the *arguments* are passed through a shell before they are passed to the subprocess, allowing shell metacharacters to be used in filenames.

Set Breakpoint

b*r*c sets a breakpoint at *address*. The command *c* is executed each time the breakpoint is encountered. The breakpoint is executed (*count* − 1) times before a stop occurs. If this command sets the current address *dot* to 0, the breakpoint causes a stop.

Terminate Process

k terminates the current process, if any.

Writing Words to Memory

[?/]w *value* ... or [?/]W *value* ... writes *value* into the addressed location. *value* is 2 bytes if the command is w and 4 bytes if the command is W. Odd addresses are not permitted in writing to the subprocess address space.

Variables

Whenever the adb debugger is started, it creates a set of its own variables, setting the values of these from the system header in *corefile* unless *corefile* does not appear to be a core file, in which case these values are set from *objfile* (see *corefile* and *objfile* in the "Options and Arguments" section below). The variables are set to the addresses and sizes of the various parts of the program file as follows:

Variable	Definition
b	base address of the data segment
d	data segment size
e	entry address of program
m	execution type
n	number of segments
s	stack segment size
t	text segment size

The above-named variables are set by *adb* initially, but they are not used afterward.

Numbered variables are used for communication as follows:

0 indicates the last value printed.
1 is the last offset part of an instruction source.
2 is the previous value of variable.

Addresses

Addresses under adb are either file or memory locations. If a current process is in memory, such as following execution of a :r command, addresses are taken to be memory locations. Otherwise, adb addresses are file locations and any requested text or data are read from *objfile* or *corefile*.

Every text or data segment in a program has a memory map entry associated with it. Each memory map entry has a unique *segment_number*: the *file position* of the segment's first byte and the *physical_size* of the segment in the file.

If a process is executing, the memory location is the *offset* in the specified segment, where the *offset* must be positive, but no larger than *size* (*size* is physical size for file locations and virtual size for memory locations) in order for *address* to be legal. If no process is executing but an *address* is specified, the file location that corresponds to that *address* is equal to the *file_position* plus the *offset*.

Initial address mappings are suitable for operations with normal a.out and core files. If the files are not normal a.out and core files, *size* is set to the maximum file size, and *file position* is set to 0 so that the whole file may be examined without address translation. All appropriate address values are signed 32-bit integers so that *adb* can operate on large files.

Register Names
80286 Registers

ax	accumulator
bx	base
cx	counter
dx	data
bp	base pointer
sp	stack pointer
si	source index
di	destination index
cs	code segment
ds	data segment
es	extra segment
ss	stack segment
fl	flags register
ip	instruction pointer

Expressions

Expressions in *adb* may contain *adb* variables; decimal, octal, and hexadecimal integers; register names; symbols; and various arithmetic and logical operators, including the following:

Operands

" is the last *address* entered.

+ is the value of *dot* incremented by the current increment.

^ is the value of *dot* decremented by the current decrement.

. is the value of *dot*, the current position in the file.

'*cccc*' is the ASCII value of as many as four characters. An apostrophe character (') can be escaped by using a backslash (\).

(*exp*) is the value of expression *exp*.

integer is octal if *integer* begins with 0, hexadecimal if it begins with # or 0x. Otherwise, it is decimal.

integer.fraction is a 32-bit floating point number.

<*name* is the value of *name* (a register name or one of the variable names maintained by *adb*). If *name* is a register name, the register value is obtained from the *corefile* system header. The permissible register names are ax, bx, cx, dx, si, bp, fl, cs, ds, ss, es, and sp. See "Register Names" above.

symbol is a sequence of letters (upper- or lowercase), digits, or underscores not starting with a digit. The *symbol* value is taken from the symbol table in *objfile*. If an initial underscore (_) or ~ is needed, it will be prepended to the *symbol*.

_*symbol* begins with an underscore if it is the true name (in the C language) of an external symbol. This distinguishes the symbol from the internal or hidden variables of a program.

Monadic Operators

*exp gets the contents of the location addressed by *exp*.

−*exp* performs integer negation.

~*exp* gets the bitwise complement.

Dyadic Operators

Dyadic operators bind more tightly than monadic operators. Also, dyadic operators are left-associative. The actions of the dyadic operators are as follows:

e1 + e2	integer addition
e1 − e2	integer subtraction

*e1*e2*	integer multiplication
e1%e2	integer division
e1&e2	bitwise conjunction
e1|e2	bitwise disjunction
e1^e2	gets the remainder after division of *e1* by *e2*.
e1#e2	rounds *e1* up to the next multiple of *e2*.

Options and Arguments

−p *prompt* defines *prompt*, the string that adb presents to the user. The prompt may be any string of characters. The default *prompt* is an asterisk (*). Enclose the prompt string in quotation marks if it contains spaces. At least one space must separate −p and *prompt*.

−w causes both *corefile* and *objfile* to be created, if neccesary, and opened for both reading and writing so that adb can modify the files.

corefile is the name of the core image file produced by the system after executing *objfile*. The default name for *corefile* is core. Core image files have the contents of CPU registers, the stack, and program memory areas.

objfile is the file to be debugged or examined. Ordinarily it is an executable file that has a COFF or XENIX format and contains a symbol table. The default name for *objfile* is a.out.

outfile is the name of a data file which adb is to examine.

Files

```
a.out
core
```

See Also

a.out (SCO 1988j), core (SCO 1988j), ptrace (Peterson 1991)

Diagnostic Messages

The exit status of adb is 0 unless the last command returned non-zero status or failed.

The adb command reports abnormal termination of commands, inaccessible files, syntax error, and so on.

If there is no current command or format, the message 'adb' is displayed.

Warning Notes

It is impossible to single-step system calls.

If a breakpoint is set at the entry point of a program, it will have no effect on initial entry to the program.

If a local variable has the same name as an external variable, it may make the external variable inaccessible.

admin (CP)   SOURCE CODE CONTROL SYSTEM   admin (CP)

Name

admin—create SCCS files or alter SCCS file parameters

Synopsis

admin [-n] [-i[*filename*]] [-r*rel*] [-f*flag*[*flagval*]] [-d*flag*[*flagval*]]   [-a*login*]   [-e*login*]   [-m[*mrlist*]] [-y[*comment*]] [-h] [-z] *files*

Description

The admin command creates new SCCS s-files (see the "Files" section below) or changes parameters of existing SCCS s-files. Text controlled by SCCS must be interpretable by the editors ed and vi. Files named by admin are created if they do not exist. SCCS file parameters are initialized as specified by arguments of the command. If no initial value is specified for an argument, a default value is assigned. If a file specified by admin already exists, parameters specified by admin are changed; other parameters remain the same.

When a directory is named in admin, each file in the directory is processed by admin, except that non-SCCS files (filenames that do not end in .s) and unreadable files are ignored. If − is given as the name following the −i argument, each line of standard input is taken to be the name of an SCCS file to be processed by admin; non-SCCS files and unreadable files are ignored.

The admin command uses a transient lock file (z.filename) to prevent simultaneous updates of an SCCS file by different users (see get (CP) for additional details).

SCCS filenames must start with the character s, and the last part of any SCCS file name must be s.*filename*.

Newly created SCCS files are assigned mode 444 [chmod (Peterson 1992)]. Any writing by admin is sent to a temporary file, x.*filename* [see get (CP)]. The temporary file is created with the same mode as the SCCS file if the SCCS file already exists, or with mode 444 if a new SCCS file is being created. If admin executes successfully, the SCCS file is deleted and x.*filename* is renamed with the name of the SCCS file. Thus an SCCS file is modified only if no errors occurred.

Any directories containing SCCS files should have mode 444. The mode of the directories prevents anyone except the owner from changing SCCS files contained in the directories. The mode of the SCCS files prevents any changes except by using SCCS commands.

The mode of an SCCS file should be changed to 644 if the file must be patched. This allows ed to be used. After editing, the file should be examined for corruption by using admin −h. Next, admin −z should be executed to compute a checksum. Finally, admin −h should be executed again to ensure that the SCCS file is valid.

Options and Arguments

Arguments to admin may appear in any order. These arguments consist of keyletter arguments beginning with a hyphen (−) or filenames. The effects of arguments apply independently to each named file.

−a*login* specifies a *login* name or a numerical XENIX group ID to be added to the list of users authorized to make changes (deltas) to the SCCS file. More than one −a keyletter may be used on the command line of a single admin command. Also, the list may simultaneously have as many *login*s or group IDs as desired. Specifying a group ID has the effect of specifying all of the *login* names common to that group ID. Anyone may add deltas if no list of users is specified.

−d*flag* deletes the specified *flag* from an SCCS file. More than one −d keyletter may be used on the command line of an *admin* command. The −d keyletter can only be specified for an SCCS file that already exists. See the −f keyletter for permissible *flag* names.

l*list* gives a *list* of releases to be unlocked. See the documentation for the −f keyletter for the syntax of *list* and for a description of l.

−e*login* deletes a *login* name or numerical group ID from the list of users allowed to make deltas to an SCCS file. More than one −e keyletter may be used on the command line of a single admin command. Specifying a group ID deletes all of the *login* names common to that group ID.

−f*flag*[*flagval*] specifies a *flag* and, optionally, a value for *flag*, *flagval*, to be inserted in the SCCS file. More than one −f may appear on the command line of a single admin command. The *flag*s and their permissible values are as follows:

b lets the get (CP) command create branch deltas.

c*ceil* sets the highest release number (ceiling) which may be retrieved by a get (CP) command for editing. The ceiling must be greater than 0 but less than or equal to 9999. The default is 9999 when *ceil* is not specified.

d*SID* sets the default SID number used by a get (CP) command. See delta (CP) for a definition of the SID number.

f*floor* sets a minimum value, *floor*, for the number of the release which may be retrieved by a get (CP) command for editing. The *floor* must be greater than 0 but less than or equal to 9999. The default is 1 when f is unspecified.

i treats the "No id keywords (ge6)" message issued by get (CP) or delta (CP) as a fatal error. (The message is issued when SCCS identification keywords are not found in text stored or retrieved in an SCCS file.) Otherwise, the message is treated as a warning.

j allows multiple concurrent updates to the same version of an s-file. This option can cause file corruption if it is used carelessly.

l*list* lists releases for which deltas are no longer allowed. The *list* has syntax as follows:

$$<list> ::= <range> | <list>, <range>$$
$$<range>::= Release Number|a$$

Putting a in *list* specifies all releases of the named file. The get −e command fails when it is used with one of the releases specified in *list*.

m*module* gives the module name of the SCCS file to be substituted for the %M% keyword in the SCCS file text retrieved by get (CP). The default value of *module* if m is not specified is the name of the SCCS file with the leading s. deleted.

n makes delta (CP) create a "null" delta for each release that is to be skipped when a delta is made (for example, making delta 6.1 after delta 2.5 skips releases 3, 4, and 5). Any releases skipped no longer exist in the SCCS file. No branch delta can later be created from such a release.

q*text* specifies *text* to be substituted wherever the %Q% keyword occurs in an SCCS file gotten by get (CP).

t*type* specifies the *type* of module in the SCCS file substituted wherever the %Y% keyword occurs in SCCS file text gotten by get (CP).

v[*pgm*] makes delta ask for Modification Request (MR) numbers as the cause for making a delta. If v*pgm* is used when an SCCS file is being created, the m keyletter must be used too, even if its value is null. The optional value, *pgm*, gives the name of an optional validity checking program for MR numbers [see delta (CP).]

−h checks the structure of an s-file and compares a newly computed checksum with a checksum stored in the first line of the file. The checksum is the sum of all of the characters in the SCCS file except the characters in the first line of the SCCS file.

−i[*filename*] gives the *filename* of the file from which to take text for a new SCCS file. The text is the first delta of the file. Only one SCCS file may be created by admin if −i is used. If −i is used, −n also must be used.

If −i is omitted, the SCCS file is created empty. If −i is used but *filename* is omitted, text is gotten by reading the standard input until an EOF is found.

−m[*mrlist*] inserts an *mrlist* of MR numbers into the SCCS s-file as a reason for creating the initial delta. If −m[mrlist] is set, the −v *flag* also must be set, and *flag* must be the name of a program that validates MR numbers. If the −v *flag* is not set or validation of MR numbers fails, admin issues error messages.

−n creates a new SCCS s-file.

−r*rel* gives the initial release number for a new s-file into which the initial delta is inserted. The initial release is 1 if −r is not used. −r*rel* may be used only if −i also is used.

−y[*comment*] puts *comment* text into the SCCS a-file as a comment for the initial delta. The result is identical to that of delta. This argument is valid only if a new SCCS file is being created (−i or −n is used). The default when −y is not specified is insertion of the following comment: "date and time created YY/MM/DD HH:MM:SS by *login*."

−z recomputes the SCCS s-file checksum and stores it in the first line of the SCCS s-file. See −h above. Using −z on a corrupted file may prevent detection of the file corruption.

files specifies s-files which are to be created or which already exist and are to be modified.

Files

See get (CP) for additional details about SCCS files.

d-file is a temporary copy of the g-file, created during delta execution and deleted afterward.

g-file contains changes to be made to an original s-file. It exists before delta execution and is gone after *delta* execution is complete.

p-file contains the *SID* of the file being updated, the next *SID* when the g-file is restored to the s-file, and the *login* of the user retrieving the g-file. It exists before delta execution and may remain afterward.

q-file is used by delta when it is updating a p-file. It is created during delta execution and deleted afterward.

s-file is the primary SCCS file, holding the original file and deltas to it. Its filename is of the form s.*filename*.

x-file is created whenever changes are made to an s-file. All actual changes are made to the x-file, holding the s-file safe in case of a crash. The existing s-file is replaced by the x-file when changes are finished. The x-file is created with read-only permission if admin is creating a new file, or with the same mode as the SCCS file if it already exists.

z-file is a transient lock file that prevents simultaneous s-file updates by different users. It contains the process ID of the currently executing SCCS process.

See Also

cdc (CP), comb (CP), delta (CP), get (CP), help (CP), prs (CP), rmdel (CP), sact (CP), sccsdiff (CP), unget (CP), val (CP), vc (CP), what (CP), ed (SCO 1988j)

---

ar (CP)   **LIBRARY MANAGEMENT**   **ar (CP)**

Name

ar - maintain archive files

Synopsis

ar *key* [*positname*] *archfile names* . . .

Description

The main purpose of ar is to create and update groups of files that are combined into one XENIX format archive file. Archive files are mainly used as libraries by the link editor and various compilers. The command can combine several files into one archive file. The files may be any combination of object files or COFF files.

A file may be put in the archive twice if it is mentioned twice in the ar argument list.

Libraries must be processed or reprocessed with ranlib (CP); otherwise, ld (CP) will fail. Phase errors are possible because generation of a library and randomization by ranlib are separate.

The loader, ld, warns if the modification date of a library is more recent than the creation of its dictionary. However, the warning appears even if the library is only being copied.

Options and Arguments

The operation of the ar command is determined by a command key and by command options. The command key, *key*, is a mandatory part of the command line. It may begin with a hyphen. It consists of one of the letters dmpqrtx, described below. Optionally, the *keyarg* may be concatenated with one or more letters from the set vuaibcln.

c suppresses the message produced by default when *archfile* is created.

d removes the named files from the archive file.

l puts temporary files in the current working (local) directory instead of in /tmp, the default temporary directory.

m is a positioning character that moves the named files to the end of the archive. The *positname* argument must be present when a positioning character is present. As in r, it must tell where the files are to be moved.

p prints the named files in the archive.

q quickly appends named files to the end of the archive. The optional positioning characters a, b, and i are not valid. No checking is done to determine whether added files are already in the archive. The q option avoids quadratic behavior in building a large archive file by file.

r replaces named files in the archive. If the *keyarg* u is used with r, archive files are replaced only when they have modification dates earlier than the modification dates of replacement files. New files are placed after *positname* if the *keyarg* a is concatenated with r, or before *positname* if *keyarg*s b or i are concatenated with r.

t prints a table of contents of the archive file. The names of all files in the archive are put in the table if no names are specified. Otherwise, only the names given are tabled.

v gives a verbose, file-by-file report of the generation of a new archive file from an old archive file and constituent files. A long listing of all information about files is given if t is used with v. Each file must be preceded by a name if x is used with v.

x extracts the specified files. All files are extracted if no names are given. The x argument never modifies a file.

archfile is the name of the archive.

names specifies constituent files of the archive.

positname is the file that is used as a reference point when other files are positioned in the archive.

Files

/tmp/v* contains temporary files

See Also

ld (CP), lorder (CP), nm (CP), strip (CP), tsort (CP), a.out (SCO 1988j), ar (SCO 1988j), tmpnam (Peterson 1992)

Name

asx—XENIX 8086/186/286 assembler

Synopsis

asx[*options*] *source_file*

Description

asx, also known as the Ritchie assembler, assembles 8086/186/286 source files and creates linkable object modules. It was used before the cmerge C compiler was introduced, and is not compatible with cc (CP). This assembler should not be used for new development; use masm (CP), the supported XENIX assembler, instead.

asx accepts a single file as input (see the *source_file* argument below) and produces a single file as output (see the −o *filename* option below).

asx recognizes only 8086 instruction mnemonics. If instructions for the 80186, 80286, 8087, or 80287 chip are to be assembled, the source file must contain the corresponding .286c, .286p, .8087, or .287 assembler directive.

Use the ld (CP) linker to link object modules produced by asx.

Options and Arguments

−a causes assembled segments to be output in alphabetic order, rather than in order of occurrence in the source file.

−d generates program listings for both assembler passes. These two listings permit phase errors between assembler passes to be resolved. Unless the −l option is used, the −d option is ignored.

−l creates a listing file that has the same base name as the source file, but also has a .lst extension.

−Mu makes uppercase and lowercase letters in all names and symbols indistinguishable to the assembler by disabling case sensitivity. The −Mu option causes all symbols defined by EXTERN and PUBLIC directives to be output in uppercase.

−Mx makes uppercase and lowercase letters in all names and symbols (except symbols defined in EXTERN and PUBLIC directives) indistinguishable to the assembler by disabling case sensitivity. This option causes all symbols defined by EXTERN and PUBLIC directives to be output with their original case.

−n prevents creation of the symbol table in the program listing.

−o *filename* specifies the object module generated by asx. No default file extension is appended to the specified *filename*. If no *filename* is specified, the default filename is *source_file*, the base name of the file containing the input file. The object module gets an .o file extension.

−O causes program values in the listing to be displayed in octal. The default radix for display of values is decimal.

−r generates actual 8087/80287 instructions for floating point computation. Object modules generated using the −r option can be executed only on machines that have an 8087 or 80287 coprocessor. The default option is to generate software interrupts to enable the use of a floating point emulation package.

−X causes the assembler to list any conditional block that has an IF condition that evaluates to "false." This option is ignored unless the −l option is in effect. The .TFCOND directive can override this option.

source_file is the file which asx accepts as input. The file must have an .s extension.

Files

/bin/asx

See Also

ld (CP)

---

cb (CP)	DEBUGGING AIDS	cb (CP)

Name

cb—C program beautifier

Synopsis

cb [−s] [−j] [−l *length*] [*filename* ...]

Description

The cb command reads C code from the specified file(s) or from standard input if *filename* is not specified and writes the code to the standard output after formatting it to display its structure. If no command line options are given, the specified files are structured so that braces align vertically and code within braces is indented one tab stop. Any punctuation hidden in preprocessor statements will cause indentation errors.

Options and Arguments

$-j$ rejoins lines that have been split.

$-l$ *length* splits lines that are longer than *length*.

$-s$ standardizes the style of code to match that in *The C Programming Language* by Kernighan and Ritchie.

filename is the file containing C programs to be beautified. Several files may be specified.

See Also

cc (CP)

Kernighan, B.W. & D.M. Ritchie. 1978. *The C Programming Language.* Englewood Cliffs, NJ: Prentice-Hall.

cc (CP)	C COMPILATION	cc (CP)

Name

cc—C compiler

Synopsis

cc [*options*] *filenames* . . .

Description

cc is the XENIX C compiler command for creating executable programs by compiling and linking specified files. cc invokes the C compiler for each C source file (see *filenames* under "Options and Arguments" below) and compiles the resulting object code to a file having the same basename as the source code file, but with an .o extension. cc invokes masm, the XENIX assembler, to process assembler source code (see *filenames* under "Options and Arguments" below), and it copies the resulting object code to a file having the same basename as the source code file, but with an .o extension.

The compiler, cc, does nothing to object or library files until it has compiled or assembled all source files. It then invokes ld, the XENIX link editor, to form a single program by combining all object files it has generated together with object files and libraries specified on the command line.

cc sets the entry point of each program to the beginning of standard startup code that calls the main() function of the program.

cc processes files in the order in which they are specified on the command line. It examines library files only if functions referenced in previous files are not yet defined, except that *cc* automatically searches a number of standard libraries that support C library functions and program startup routines. Functions that define unresolved references are the only ones that are concatenated.

The first member of each library file must be named __.SYMDEF, that is, the file must be in ranlib (CP) format. Every object module library must have a current ranlib directory. The most recent library versions must have been processed by ranlib; otherwise, ld will be unable to create executable programs that use such libraries.

Memory Models

The program's memory model determines which libraries will be used; based on the configuration option, cc automatically selects the correct versions of standard libraries for small, middle, large, and huge models. User must ensure that their own object files and private libraries are compiled using the correct model. Five different memory models are available: small, middle, compact, large, and huge. Small models can be either pure or impure. Small, middle, large, and huge models can be linked only with library and object files of the same model.

Special calls and returns are used with the middle, large, and huge programs. These increase execution time.

Function pointers in middle, large, and huge models are 32 bits long. Data pointers in large and huge model programs are 32 bits long. Be careful to avoid incorrect use of these pointers.

The middle, large, and huge segmentation models are used with 8086 or 80286 processors. They allow programs with code or data larger than 64K bytes. The middle, large, and huge models are not supported on the 80386, since the 80386 can address segments larger than 64K bytes.

The −ND, −NM, or −NT options (see "Options and Arguments below) may be used to send text and data of specified object files to designated physical segments. This way, all text having the same name is sent to the same physical segment.

Impure-Text Small Model

Impure-text small model programs occupy a single 64K-byte segment which contains all program text and data. This is the default model, but the −Ms option will create this model, too.

Pure-Text Small Model

Pure-text small model programs occupy two 64K-byte segments, with text and data in separate segments. Text is read-only. It may be shared by several processes at one time. Use −Mm and −i to create pure-text model programs.

Middle Model

Middle model programs occupy several segments, but data may occupy only one segment. Data cannot exceed 64K bytes. Text may occupy as many segments as neccessary and may be of any size. Special calls and returns access functions in other text segments. Middle model programs are always pure. Use the −Mm option to create middle model programs.

Compact Model

Compact model programs may have multiple segments of data, possibly exceeeding 64K bytes, but text must not exceed 64K bytes. Use the −Mc option to create compact model programs.

Large Model

Large model programs may occupy several segments. Both text and data may occupy as many segments as necessary. Special addresses are used to access data in other data segments. Special calls and returns access functions in other text segments. No single data item may exceed 64K bytes, but text and data may be of any size. Large model programs are always pure. Use the −Ml option to create large model programs.

Huge Model

Huge model programs may occupy more than one physical segment. Both text and data may occupy as many segments as necessary, and a data construct may span 64K-byte segments, but this model imposes limits on the way a data construct is formed and on where it is placed in memory. Huge model programs are always pure. Use the −Mh option to create huge model programs.

Options and Arguments

The compiler, cc, reads /etc/default/cc to get information about default options and libraries (see the "Files" section below for details). The options are as follows:

−a is passed directly to the loader. See ld (CP).

−c suppresses link editing and does not remove object files that may be created. No executable program is created.

−C prevents comments from being stripped from a file that is being preprocessed. This option works only when used with −E, −P, or EP.

−compat makes an executable file binary compatible on the following systems:

XENIX-286 System V
XENIX-386 System V

XENIX-286 3.0
XENIX-8086 System V

−CSON (or −CSOFF) enables (or disables) common subexpression optimization when optimization (−O) is specified.

−d displays preprocessor passes and arguments before execution.

−D*name*[=*string*] defines *name* to the preprocessor as though *name* were defined by a #define statement in each source file. If no *string* is specified, *name* is 1. Otherwise, *name* equals *string*.

−dos makes cc create a program able to run under MS-DOS.

−E preprocesses each source file, then copies the result to the standard output. −E also puts a #line directive with the current input line number and source file name at the start of output for each file.

−EP works like −E, except that −EP does not put a #line directive at the start of each file.

−F *num* sets the program stack size to *num* (hexadecimal) bytes. The default stack size for the 80286, 1000, (hexadecimal) bytes. The default stack size for the 8086, 1000, is variable. It starts at the top of a 64K-byte data segment that grows downward until it reaches data. The 80386 has a variable stack, so this option does not apply.

−Fa (or −Fa*name*) creates and puts an assembly source listing in *source*.s (or in the named file, *name*). The link continues if the user requests it.

−Fc (or −Fc*name*) creates and puts a merged assembly and a C source listing in *source*.L (or in the named file, *name*).

−Fe*name* names the executable file, *name*.

−Fl (or −Fl*name*) creates and puts a listing in *source*.L (or in the named file, *name*) with assembly source and object code. The link continues if the user requests it.

−Fm (or −Fm*name*) instructs the linker to put a map listing in a.map (or in the named file, *name*). The file contains the names of all the segments in the order in which they appear in the load module.

−Fo*name* names the object file *name* instead of source.o.

−FPa, −FPc, −FPc87, −FPi, or FPi87 controls the type of floating point code generated and tells which library support is to be used. The −dos option must be used with these options. The default option is −FPi.

−Fs (or −Fs*name*) creates and puts a C source listing in *source*.s (or in the named file, *name*).

−g causes the compiler to generate symbol table information needed by the symbolic debugger, sdb (CP). This option has the same effect as the −Z*i* option.

−help prints the help menu.

−HELP prints the help menu.

−H*num* makes *num* the maximum length of external symbols. This option has the same effect as the −n1 option.

−i makes the instruction space of a small model program separate from its data space. The program text and data areas are allocated separate physical segments when the output file is executed. The text (instructions) is read-only; it may be shared by all users executing the file. The middle model or large model implies the use of this option. The −i option is not implemented on every brand of machine.

−I*pathname* adds *pathname* to the list of directories to be searched if an #include file is not found in the directory that contains the current source file or if angle brackets (<>) enclose the filename. Directories in a standard list are searched if the file cannot be found in directories in the list of directories to be searched.

−K deletes stack probes from a program. These stack probes are used to detect stack overflow if it occurs on entry to program routines. Since code generated for the 80386 does not require stack probes, this option has no effect if −M3 is used.

−L creates a listing of assembly source code and assembled code, and puts it in a file that has the same basename as the source code file but a .L extension. This option suppresses the −S option.

−LARGE is executable only on 286 or 386 processors. It invokes the compiler's large model passes. This option should be used if "out of heap space" errors occur.

−link enables the user to specify linker switches at compile time that are not supported by the driver. Any text options and filenames that follow the −link option are passed to the linker directly. If used, this option must appear last on the command line.

−l*name* searches the specified library, *name*, for any unresolved function references.

−M *string* sets the configuration of the program, determining the memory model, word order, and data threshold of the program. It enables such C language enhancements as keywords and advanced instruction sets. *string* may consist of any combination of the following characters, except that "s", "m", "l", and "h" below are mutually exclusive. Any size specifier used (c, s, m, l, or h) must appear after any code type specifier used (0, 1, 2, or 3), for example, −M2m.

a restricts code to ANSI specifications.

c generates a compact model program (286 compilation only).

e enables certain non-ANSI C extensions necessary to maintain compatibility with existing versions of the C compiler. It also enables these keywords: far, near, huge, pascal, and fortran.

h generates a huge model program.

s generates a small model program (default).

l generates a large model program (286 compilation only).

m generates a middle model program (286 compilation only).

0 enables generation of 8086 code. Valid size specifiers are s, m, and l·

1 enables generation of 186 code. Valid size specifiers are s, m, and l.

2 enables generation of 286 code. Valid size specifiers are s, m, and l.

3 enables generation of 386 code. Valid size specifiers are s, m, and l.

b reverses the word order of type long variables; the default is the low-order word first.

d tells the compiler not to assume that the SS register equals the DS register.

f enables software floating point computation, although it does not exist in XENIX. This is useful in compiling object files to be linked on MS-DOS.

t *size* sets the threshold for the size of the largest item in the data group to *size* (default: 32,767). This option is to be used only with large model programs.

−m *name* creates a map file, *name*. This option has the same effect as −Fm.

−n sets the pure text model (i.e., not both data and text). Using this option is equivalent to using the −i option. It warns that −i is being set.

−ND *name* makes *name* the data segment name of each compiled or assembled source file. the name "_DATA" is used if _ND is not specified.

−nl *leng* makes the maximum length of external symbols be *leng*. Any names longer than *leng* are truncated before they are copied to the external symbol table.

−NM *name* makes *name* be the module name of each compiled or assembled source file. If −NT *name* is not used, the filename of each source file is used.

−NT *name* makes *name* be the text segment name of each compiled or assembled source file. If −NT *name* is not used, the name "*module*_TEXT" is used for middle model programs and "_TEXT is used for small model programs. Do not use this option with 386 code.

−o *outfile* produces an output object file named *outfile*. The default *outfile* is a.out. *outfile* cannot end in .o or .c.

−O *string* optimizes object code. *string* may be one or more of the following characters:

a relaxes alias checking.

c deletes common expressions (80386 only).

d disables all optimization.

l does various loop optimizations (80386 only).

p optimizes precision.

s optimizes code to reduce space.

t optimizes code to increase speed (default). It is equivalent to the −O option.

x does maximum optimization. It is quivalent to the −Oactl option.

−p causes the compiler to add code to count the number of times each routine is called. When object program execution terminates normally, the mon.out file is produced. It contains execution counts. Thereafter, prof (CP) can produce an execution profile.

−P runs only cpp (CP) on the specified C programs, putting the result in corresponding files with .i suffixes.

−pack packs structures, storing each structure member in the first available byte, no matter what the int boundaries are. Extra time will be required to access 16-bit members that begin on odd boundaries, thus slowing execution of code.

−r invokes the incremental linker, /lib/ldr.

−s tells the linker to strip all symbol table information from the executable output file.

−S makes an assembly source listing in a file with the same basename as the source file, but with a .s extension. The resulting file is unsuitable for assembly. The code is intended only for reading.

−SEG num establishes num as the maximum number of segments a linker can process (range: 1 to 1024 segments). Use the −NT option to reduce the number of segment names if 1024 is too small.

−u deletes all manifest defines. See the −U option below.

−U definition deletes or undefines the specified manifest define. The possible manifest defines are as follows:

M_BITFIELDS
M_I86
M_I8086 or M_I186 or M_I286 or M_I386
M_I86M_ or M_I86MM or M_I86LM
M_SDATA or M_LDATA
M_STEXT or M_LTEXT
M_SYS3 or M_SYSIII
M_SYS5 or M_SYSV
M_WORDSWAP
M_XENIX

−V num tells under which version of XENIX the file is to be executed. The values of num can be 2, 3, or 5. Any other value causes a fatal error. The default is −V5 if this option is not specified. The −V num option determines the version name sent to the preprocessor to indicate the target XENIX system as follows:

$\quad$ −V2 defines M_V7.

$\quad$ −V3 defines M_SYS3.

$\quad$ −V5 defines both M_SYS3 and M_SYS5.

$\quad$ −w suppresses compiler warning messages. It has the same effect as the −W 0 option.

$\quad$ −W *num* determines the output level of compiler warning messages. No warning messages are issued if *num* is 0. Only warnings about program structure and overt type mismatches are issued if *num* is 1. If *num* is 2, then warnings about strong type mismatches are issued. If *num* is 3, then warnings for all automatic conversions are issued. Compiler error messages are unaffected by this option.

$\quad$ −X deletes standard directories from the list of directories to be searched for #include files.

$\quad$ −z displays the various passes, together with their arguments, without executing them.

$\quad$ −Za restricts the generated code to ANSI specifications. This option has the same effect as −Ma.

$\quad$ −Zd puts line number information in the object file.

$\quad$ −Ze enables the following keywords: far, near, huge, pascal, and fortran. This option has the same effect as −Me.

$\quad$ −Zg produces function declarations from function definitions. It writes declarations to standard output. It causes p2, p3, and ld to be omitted.

$\quad$ −Zi puts information used by the symbolic debugger (sdb) in the output file. This option has the same effect as −g.

$\quad$ −Zl deletes library information from the object file.

$\quad$ −Zp*n* packs structure members in memory, allocating alignment to 1 for 8086 processors. The *n* argument can be as follows:

$\quad\quad$ 1 allocates alignment to 1.

$\quad\quad$ 2 allocates alignment to 2 (default for 80286 programs).

$\quad\quad$ 3 allocates alignment to 4 (default for 80386 programs).

$\quad$ −Zs omits p2, p3, and ld386, performing a syntax check only.

$\quad$ *filenames* specifies files to be compiled: C source files (.c extension) or assembler source files (.s extension) and files to be linked: object files (.o extension) or library files (.a extension).

Files

$\quad$ /bin/cc contains the driver.

$\quad$ /lib/p0, p1, p2, p3 contains the small model passes.

$\quad$ /lib/p1L, p2L, p3L contains the large model passes.

/lib/*.a contains the standard libraries.

/etc/default/cc contains the default options and libraries. The default file may contain lines such as the following:

FLAGS =

or

LIBS =

cc treats any parameters that follow FLAGS = as if they had been given at the start of the command line. This allows, among other things, the specification of more libraries. cc always searches for some file in /etc/default/cc matching the last component of the pathname used to invoke cc. Thus different defaults may be selected by linking cc to different names and invoking cc by the name that is linked to the desired defaults.

See Also

asx (CP), cpp (CP), ld (CP), lint (CP), masm (CP), prof (CP), ranlib (CP), sdb (CP), machine (SCO 1988h). Also, see *XENIX System V Development System: C Language Guide* (SCO 1988a), *XENIX System V Development System: C Language Reference* (SCO 1988b, and *XENIX System V Development System: C Library Guide* (SCO 1988c).

cdc (CP)   SOURCE CODE CONTROL SYSTEM   cdc (CP)

Name

cdc—change delta commentary in SCCS s-file(s)

Synopsis

cdc −r*SID* [−m[*mrlist*]] [−y[*comments*]] *filenames*

Description

The cdc command changes the delta commentary of each SCCS file specified in the cdc command line that has the SCCS Identification string (*SID*) specified in the −r option. The delta commentary is the comment and Modification Request (MR) number previously specified by the −m and −y arguments of the delta (CP) command.

Permission to change the delta commentary requires permission to make the delta in the first place. Changing the delta commentary requires ownership of both the file and the directory.

Text controlled by SCCS files must be interpretable by the editors ed and vi.

Options and Arguments

The following arguments consist of options and filenames. The options may appear in any order, and each applies independently to each file named:

−m*mrlist* specifies a list of MR entries to be deleted if they already exist or to be added if they do not already exist. A null list of MRs has no effect. The MRs in an MR list must be separated by blanks and/or tab characters. Any newline character ends the MR list unless the newline is preceded by an escape character.

If an SCCS s-file has its v flag set [see v in admin (CP)], it is possible to supply a list of MR numbers to be deleted and/or added in the delta commentary of the *SID* specified by −r. If the v flag has a value assigned, it is treated as the name of a shell procedure or program for validating MR numbers. The cdc command terminates without changing the delta commentary if the validation program returns a nonzero exit status.

A ! character in front of the MR number of any MR entry indicates that it is to be deleted. The cdc command causes any deleted MRs to be listed in the comment section of the delta commentary, preceded by a comment line saying that the MRs have been deleted. The cdc command adds MR entries to the MR list in the same way that the admin (CP) command does.

The MRs? prompt is sent to the standard output before the standard input is read if the standard input is a terminal and if the −m argument is not used. No prompt is sent if the standard output is not a terminal.

The −m argument (and the −y argument) must be used if SCCS file names are given to cdc on the command line (standard input).

−r*SID* specifies the *SID* of a delta that is to have its delta commentary changed. The −r argument always specifies a *SID* in any SCCS command.

−y*comments* gives a new *comments* string that replaces old comment string(s) for the delta specified by −r. The old *comments* are retained, preceded by a line announcing that they have been changed.

The −y argument must be used if SCCS filenames are given to cdc on the command line (standard input). The comments? prompt is sent to standard output before standard input is read if −y is not given and if the standard input is a terminal. No prompt is sent if the standard input is not a terminal. The comments? prompt is always preceded by an MRs? prompt.

˙Null *comments* have no effect. A newline character will terminate *comments* text unless the newline character is preceded by an escape character.

filenames names the SCCS s-file(s) which will have delta commentary changed. If *filenames* is −, cdc treats each line of the standard input as the name of an SCCS file to be processed. If *filenames* is −, the −m and −y options must be used. If a directory is specified by *filenames*, then cdc treats each file in the directory as a file to be processed. However, unreadable files and files lacking a .s prefix are ignored.

Files

See the "Files" subsection of the *get* (CP) command for a description of all SCCS files.

x-file See admin (CP), delta (CP), and get (CP).

z-file See delta (CP), and get (CP).

See Also

admin (CP), cdc (CP), comb (CP), delta (CP), get (CP), help (CP), prs (CP), rmdel (CP), sact (CP), sccsdiff (CP), unget (CP), val (CP), vc (CP), what (CP), sccsfile (SCO 1988j)

cflow (CP)	C DEBUGGING AIDS	cflow (CP)

Name

cflow—make a C flowgraph charting external references

Synopsis

cflow [−r] [−ix] [−i__] [−d*num*] *filenames*

Description

cflow tells which procedures are called by other procedures. It can analyze a collection of assembler, C, lex, object, and yacc files, converting information extracted from symbol tables into a graph of external references, which is then displayed on the standard output.

Each line of standard output consists of a reference number, some number of tabs indicating the nesting level, the name of a global procedure, a colon, and the definition of the global procedure. Ordinarily, a global procedure is a function that is not defined as external and whose name does not begin with an underscore.

For symbols derived from C source code, the symbol definition consists of a type definition (e.g., int), the name of the source file (delimited by < >), and the line number where the definition was found. Leading underscores (__) in C external names are removed.

After the definition of a symbol has been printed, further references to the symbol consist of the reference number of the line where the symbol is defined. Only < > is printed for references that are undefined.

The cflow command can fail to work correctly when given files produced by lex (CP), or yacc (CP) because these commands reorder line number declarations. Give cflow (CP) the input to lex or yacc.

Options and Arguments

−D has the same action as −D in the cc (CP) and cpp (CP) commands.

−I has the same action as −I in the cc (CP) and cpp (CP) commands.

−U has the same action as −U in the cc (CP) and cpp (CP) commands.

−d*num* cuts off the graph at the specified nesting depth (*num* must be a nonnegative decimal integer). If the nesting level becomes too deep, use the −e option of pr (CP) to compress tab expansion to fewer than eight spaces.

−i_ includes procedures whose names begin with an underscore. Otherwise, these functions (and data if −ix is used) are excluded by default.

−ix includes external and static data symbols in the graph. Otherwise, only functions are included by default.

−r generates an inverted listing that shows the callers of each function, sorted in lexicographical order by callee.

filenames specifies the files to be processed by cflow. Before being processed by cflow, files with .c, .l, or .y suffixes are processed by cpp (CP), lex (CP), or yacc (CP), respectively. The results of this processing, as well as any files with .i suffixes, are next processed by the first pass of lint (CP). Files with .s suffixes are assembled and information is extracted from the symbol tables. The cflow command also extracts information from the symbol tables of any files with .o suffixes.

See Also

as (CP), cc (CP), cpp (CP), lex (CP), lint (CP), nm (CP), yacc (CP), pr (SCO 1988j)

comb (CP)   SOURCE CODE CONTROL SYSTEM   comb (CP)

Name

comb—generate a shell procedure to reconstruct SCCS files

Synopsis

comb −o −s [−p*SID*] [−c*list*] *filenames*

Description

comb creates a shell procedure that reconstructs the specified SCCS files when executed. The purpose is to make reconstructed files that are smaller than the originals.

The reconstructed file that comb creates may be larger than the original. Also, the shape of the tree of deltas may be rearranged.

Options and Arguments

Keyletter arguments may be specified in any order. If no keyletter arguments are specified, comb preserves leaf deltas and just enough ancestors to preserve the tree. Each keyletter argument applies independently to each SCCS file. If keyletter arguments are specified, they are as follows:

−c*list* instructs comb to preserve deltas in *list*. All other deltas are discarded. See get (CP) for the syntax of *list*.

−o causes the reconstructed file to be accessed at the release of the delta to be created instead of accessing the reconstructed file at the most recent ancestor (when a get −e is executed). This option may change the shape of the delta tree of the original file or decrease the size of the reconstructed SCCS file.

−p*SID* specifies the *SID* (SCCS Identification string) of the oldest delta that is to be saved. Older deltas are deleted from the reconstructed file.

−s causes comb to create a shell procedure that generates a report for each file, giving the file name, file size (number of blocks) after combination, original size (number of blocks), and percentage change in file size computed by:

$$100 * \text{(original size - combined size)}/ \text{ original size}$$

This option should be used to find out how much space will be saved if SCCS files are combined.

filenames specifies the SCCS file(s) to be reconstructed. If a filename of − is given, each line of the standard input is treated as the name of an SCCS file. Unreadable files and nonSCCS files are ignored. If a directory is specified as part of *filenames*, each file in the directory is treated as if it had been specified for processing. Again, unreadable files and nonSCCS files are ignored.

Files

See the "Files" subsection of the entry for the get (CP) command for a description of all SCCS files.

s.COMB is the reconstructed SCCS file.

comb????? is a temporary file.

See Also

admin (CP), cdc (CP), comb (CP), delta (CP), get (CP), help (CP), prs (CP), rmdel (CP), sact (CP), sccsdiff (CP), unget (CP), val (CP), vc (CP), what (CP), sccsfile (SCO 1988j), sh (SCO 1988j)

cpp (CP)	C PREPROCESSOR	cpp (CP)

Name

cpp—C language preprocessor invoked by the cc command

Synopsis

/lib/cpp [*option* . . .] [*ifile* [*ofile*]]

Description

cc automatically invokes cpp, the C language preprocessor, as the first pass in compiling C source code. Output from cpp is input to the next pass of the compiler. Since any or all of the functionality of cpp may be moved to other software in the future, cpp should not be used as a stand-alone tool. The more general preprocessor, m4 (CP), should be used when a stand-alone macroprocessor is needed.

cpp prints some self-explanatory error messages. It also prints the line number and filename where the error happened.

The current version of cpp substitutes blanks for any newlines found in the argument list. Earlier versions of cpp outputted such newlines as they were found and expanded.

Preprocessor Directives

The preprocessor, cpp, is controlled by preprocessor directives in the C source code. Each cpp directive line begins with # in column 1. Any number of tabs and blanks can be between # and a directive. Test directives and any else directives may be nested. Preprocessor directives work as follows:

#define *name definition* replaces all following occurrences of *name* by *definition*.

#define *name(arg1, . . . , argn) token-string* replaces all following occurrences of *name(arg1, . . . , argn)* by *token-string*. No spaces can be between *name* and (. Each instance of *arg* is replaced with the corresponding tokens in the list. In expanding a macro having arguments, arguments are put in the expanded *token-string* without change. When *token-string* has been expanded, cpp rescans the newly expanded token-string from the beginning, seeking names to expand.

#elif *expression* causes the following lines of C source (until the next elif, else, or endif) to be compiled if *expression* is nonzero.

#else causes the C source lines following #else to appear in the compiler output if and only if the preceding test directive condition evaluates to false (zero) and all intervening #elif conditions also equal zero.

#endif ends a group of lines begun by a test directive (#if, #ifdef, #ifndef). Test directives may be nested, but each test directive must have its own #endif. No other tokens are allowed on the #endif line.

#if *expression* causes C source lines between #if *expression* and #endif to appear in the compiler output if and only if *expression* evaluates to zero. All of the binary nonassignment C operators (, unary −, !, and the ? : operator) can be used in *expression*, with precedence the same as in C. The functionality of the #ifdef and #ifndef operators can be used in an #if directive by using the unary operator, defined, in *expression* in either of two forms: defined (*name*) or defined *name*. For example, #if defined(*x*) tests whether or not *x* is defined, as does #if defined *x*. In addition to the above operators, integer constants and names known to cpp can be used in *expression*. The sizeof operator cannot be used.

#ifdef *name* causes C source lines between #ifdef *name* and #endif to appear in the compiler output if and only if *name* has been the subject of a previous #define directive without having been the subject of an intervening #undef. No other tokens may appear after *name* on the #ifdef line.

#if defined *identifier* can be used instead of the #if directive. The directive equals 1 if *identifier* is defined, otherwise, it equals 0. Use this directive for conditional, environment-specific text.

#ifndef *name* causes C source lines between #ifdef *name* and #endif to appear in the compiler output if and only if *name* has not been the subject of a previous #define directive. No other tokens may appear after *name* on the #ifndef line.

`#include "filename"` includes the contents of *filename* in the C source at the point where `#include "filename"` appears. The directory which contains *filename* is the input file directory or the directory specified by the `-I` option.

`#include <filename>` includes the contents of *filename* in the C source at the point where `#include <filename>` appears. The directory containing *filename* is `/usr/include`. Use `#include <filename.h>` instead of an absolute pathname like `#include "/usr/include/filename.h"` because the standard directory for include files may differ in different environments. The `cpp` command gives warnings when absolute pathnames are used.

`#line integer-constant "filename"` makes `cpp` generate line control information for the next compiler pass. The line number of the next line is given by *integer-constant*, and *filename* specifies the file that contains the line. If *filename* is not specified, the current file is used. No other tokens appear on the `#line` directive line after *filename*.

`#undef name` makes *name* be forgotten for the rest of the C source code.

Options and Arguments

The `cpp` command has the following options, filenames, and special names:

`-C` causes all C comments to be sent along to the next compiler pass. Otherwise, `cpp` strips C comments by default.

`-Dname` causes *name* to be defined with a value of 1.

`-Dname=def` defines *name* as having value *def*, as if it were given by `#define`. The default value of *def* is 1. *name* will be undefined if *name* is used in both the `-D` and `-U` options because the `-U` option has a higher precedence than the `-D` option.

`-Idir` makes `cpp` search for `#include` files whose names do not begin with / first in *dir* before searching directories on the standard list. Hence, `#include` files with names enclosed in `""` are searched for first in the directory containing *ifile*, second in directories named in `-I` options, and finally in directories on a standard list. If the name of an `#include` file is enclosed in `<>`, the directory specified in *ifile* is not searched.

`-P` causes input to be preprocessed without creating line number information for the next compiler pass.

`-Uname` deletes any initial definition of *name*, where *name* is a reserved symbol that is predefined for a particular processor.

The `cpp` command understands two special names:

`_FILE_` is the current filename (a C string) known by `cpp`. It may be used like any other defined name.

__LINE_ is the current line number (decimal) known by cpp. It may be used like any other defined name.

The cpp command has two files as arguments:

ifile is the input file for cpp. The default is standard input.

ofile is the output file for cpp. The default is standard output.

Files

/usr/include is the standard directory for #include files.

See Also

cc (CP), lint (CP), m4 (CP)

---

cref (CP)	**DEBUGGING**	cref (CP)

Name

cref—make a cross-reference listing

Synopsis

cref [-acilnostux123] *files*

Description

cref makes a cross-reference listing of assembly language or C language programs. The output from cref is in four columns:

- symbol,
- filename,
- current line number or symbol, and
- text.

Options and Arguments

1 sorts output on column 1 (the default).

2 sorts output on column 2.

3 sorts output on column 3.

a makes cref use assembler format (the default).

c makes cref use C format.

i causes the next argument to be taken as an *ignore* file. The *ignore* file is a list of symbols separated by newlines. Every symbol in an *ignore* file is ignored in columns 1 and 3 of the output. This option ignores assembler predefined symbols and C language keywords. If the i option is used, the o option cannot be used. The default is i.

l puts a line number within the file to be put in column 3 instead of current symbol.

n omits column 4 (no context).

o causes the next argument to be taken as an *only* file. The *only* file is a list of symbols separated by newlines. The symbols that are in the *only* file are the only symbols that will appear in column 1 of the output. This option ignores assembler predefined symbols and C language keywords. If the o option is used, the i option cannot be used. The default is i.

s puts current symbols in column 3 (the default). In C, the current symbol is the current function name. In assembler, it is the most recently encountered name symbol.

t causes the next argument to be used as the name of the user-supplied temporary file, to be used instead of the temporary file /tmp/crt??. This file is not removed at the end of the process.

u prints only those symbols that occur once.

x prints only C external symbols.

files are the files to be searched for symbols in assembler or C syntax, as appropriate.

Files

/usr/lib/cref/* contains assembler-specific files.

See Also

as (CP), cc (CP), xref (CP), a.out (SCO 1988j)

Warning Notes

An ASCII DEL character is inserted in the intermediate file following the eighth character of each name in the source file that is eight or more characters in length.

ctags (CP)	**DEBUGGING AIDS**	ctags (CP)

Name

ctags—create a tags file for vi from C sources

Synopsis

`ctags` [-a] [-u] [-v] [-w] [-x] *filename*

Description

`ctags` generates a tags file for `vi` (SCO 1988j) from the C sources. Each line of the tags file gives a function name, the file where each function is defined, and a scanning pattern that is used to find the function definition. The `vi` command uses the tags file to find these function definitions.

The `ctags` command creates `main`, a tag given special treatment in C programs. The `ctags` command forms the tag by prepending M to the name of the file. Trailing `.c`s, if any, are removed. Leading pathname components are also removed. This processing makes it possible to use `ctags` in directories with more than one program.

Options and Arguments

The effects of the arguments are as follows:

-a appends new values for the specified files to the existing tags file.

-u removes references to the specified files in tags. Note: this option is slow.

-w suppresses warning diagnostics.

-x prints on standard output a list of function names, the filename and the line number where each function is defined, and the text of the line where each function is defined. No tags file is created when this option is used. This generates an index.

filename specifies the C source files from which `ctags` generates tags. Files with `.c` or `.h` extensions are searched for C routines and macro definitions.

Files

`tags` is the tags output file.

See Also

`ex` (SCO 1988j), `vi` (SCO 1988j)

---

cxref (CP)   **DEBUGGING AIDS**   **cxref (CP)**

Name

`cxref`—create a cross-reference table for a C program

Synopsis

cxref [*options*] *filenames*

Description

cxref builds a cross-reference table for a specified collection of C files. It puts a listing of all symbols (auto, global, static) on standard output for each file or for all files combined. Each declaring reference to a symbol is marked by an asterisk (*).

Symbols in #define statements are processed by cxref, using a special version of cpp (CP). Unfortunately, formal arguments in #define macro definitions are treated as declarations of symbols.

Options and Arguments

-D see -D option of cc (CP) or cpp (CP).

-I see -I option of cc (CP) or cpp (CP).

-U see -U option of cc (CP) or cpp (CP).

-c prints a combined cross-reference table for all input files.

-o *file* directs cxref output to the specified file.

-s suppresses printing of input filenames.

-t specifies formatting for an 80-column listing width.

-w <*num*> specifies the listing width (in decimal). The default width is 80 columns if <*num*> is not specified or is less than 51.

filenames is a collection of C files to be cross-referenced.

Files

/usr/lib contains a special version of the C-processor.

See Also

cc (CP), cpp (CP).

---

delta (CP)   SOURCE CODE CONTROL SYSTEM   delta (CP)

Name

delta—make a change (.elta) to an SCCS file

Synopsis

delta [-r*SID*] [-s] [-n] [-g*list*] [-m[*mrlist*]] [-y[*comment*]] [-p] *filenames*

Description

delta takes changes that were made to an SCCS g-file retrieved by get (CP) and puts them in an SCCS s-file. The delta command makes a delta to each file specified by *filenames*. See *filenames* under "Options and Arguments" below.

Avoid executing a get of many SCCS files followed by a single delta of those files. Use multiple get/delta sequences instead.

The SOH ASCII character (binary 001) has a special meaning to SCCS, so lines that start with the SOH character must be escaped if they are put in the SCCS file. See sccsfile (SCO 1988j) for details.

Diagnostic Messages

Error messages produced when delta aborts are of the form

ERROR *filename*: *message* (*code*)

Execute help *code* to get an explanation of the error code.

Options and Arguments

The options apply independently to each SCCS file.

−g *list* gives a list of deltas to be ignored when the SCCS file is accessed at the delta level specified for this delta.

−n causes the g-file to be kept at the end of delta processing.

−m[*mrlist*] specifies the list of Modification Request (MR) numbers given as the reason for this delta. The MR list consists of MR numbers separated by blanks and/or tabs. Any unescaped newline character terminates an MR list.

If the v flag in the SCCS file is set by the admin (C) command), an MR number must be supplied as the reason for creating a delta. If the v flag has a value, it is treated as the name of a shell procedure or program that validates MR numbers. The delta command terminates if the validation procedure returns a nonzero exit status, because delta assumes that at least one MR was invalid.

The prompt MRs? is sent to the standard output before the standard input is read if the standard output is a terminal and the −m option is not used. No prompt is sent in such a circumstance if the standard output is not a terminal. The Mr? prompt always precedes the comments? prompt (see the −y option).

−p prints on standard output in diff (SCO 1988j) format the changes (differences) in an SCCS file caused by a delta.

−r specifies which delta is to be made to an SCCS file. This option needs to be used only if the same login name has more than one get −e operation outstanding on the same SCCS file. *SID* can be the *SID* given on the get command line or the *SID* to be created as reported by get. If *SID* is omitted or is ambiguous, it is an error.

−s prevents listing (on the standard output) the newly created delta's *SID*, and the number of lines deleted, inserted, and unchanged.

−y *comment* is a string (possibly null) describing the reason for a making a delta. Any newline not preceded by an escape terminates the comment.

If the standard input is a terminal and −y is not specified, delta issues a prompt, comments?, before reading the standard input. No prompt is issued if the standard input is not a terminal. Any unescaped newline terminates the text of the comment.

filenames specifies the SCCS g-files to be used as input. If *filenames* is −, each line of the standard input is treated as the name of an SCCS g-file to be processed by delta. If the standard input (−) is specified, the −y option (and −m if necessary) must be used. Otherwise, an error occurs. If a directory is specified, delta processes each file in the directory, except that unreadable files and non-SCCS files (files lacking .s prefixes) are ignored.

Files

See admin (CP) and get (CP) for additional details about the following files:

d-file is a temporary copy of the g-file. The d-file is created during delta execution and deleted afterward.

g-file contains changes to be made to an original s-file. It exists before delta execution and is gone after delta execution is complete.

p-file contains the *SID* of the file being updated, the next *SID* when the g-file is restored to the s-file, and the *login* of the user retrieving the g-file. It exists before delta execution and may remain afterward.

q-file is used by delta when it is updating a p-file. It is created during delta execution and deleted afterward.

s-file is the primary SCCS file, holding the original file and deltas to it.

/usr/bin/bdiff computes differences between the g-file and the gotten file.

x-file is created whenever changes are made to an s-file. All actual changes are made to the x-file, holding the s-file safe in case of a crash. When changes are complete, the existing s-file is replaced by the x-file.

z-file is a lock file created to prevent simultaneous s-file updates by different users. It contains the process ID of the currently executing SCCS process.

See Also

admin (CP), cdc (CP), comb (CP), get (CP), help (CP), prs (CP), rmdel (CP), sact (CP), sccsdiff (CP), unget (CP), val (CP), vc (CP), what (CP), bdiff (SCO 1988j), sccsfile (SCO 1988j)

---

dosld (CP)   CROSS DEVELOPMENT UTILITY   dosld (CP)

Name

dosld—MS-DOS cross-linker

Synopsis

dosld [-D -H -L -M -C -F*num* -S*num* -m*filename* -nl*num*-o*filename* -u*name* -G] *filename* ...

Description

dosld links specified file(s) to create a program for execution under MS-DOS.

Options and Arguments

The options of dosld differ from those of ld (CP).

−C tells dosld not to distinguish between upper- and lowercase characters in symbol names.

−D tells dosld to perform DS allocation. This option ordinarily is used together with the −H option.

−F *num* sets the stack size to *num* (hexadecimal), the size in bytes of the stack segment in the output file.

−G tells dosld to ignore any group definitions it may find in the files. This option provides compatibility with old versions of MS-LINK. Otherwise, it should not be used.

−H tells dosld to set a field in the header of the executable file to instruct MS-DOS to load the program at the highest available memory position (Load High). This option is used with programs having data that precede code in the memory image.

−L tells dosld to include line numbers in the listing file, if any. The proper options must have been used with the compiler in order for this line number information to be available. See option −m below.

−M tells dosld to include public symbols in the list file. The symbols are sorted both lexicographically and by address. See option −m below.

−S *num* sets the segment limit to a decimal number, *num*, between 1 and 1024. This limits the number of segments that may be linked together. The higher the value of *num*, the slower the link. The default limit is 128.

−m *filename* creates a map file, *filename*, in which dosld will put information about segments and groups in the executable file. Public symbols and line numbers will be listed in *filename* if the −M and −L options are used.

−nl *num* tells dosld to truncate all public and external names that are longer than *num* (decimal) characters.

−o *filename* names the file in which dosld is to put the executable file it creates. The default is a.out.

−u *name* causes dosld to enter the specified *name* into the symbol table as an undefined symbol. This option may appear on the command line more than once. See *filename* below.

filename is the file(s) passed to dosld. The file(s) may be an ordinary 8086 object file(s), or the file(s) may be XENIX-style libraries consisting of objects collected using the ar (CP) command and indexed using the ranlib (CP) command. Libraries are searched only after all ordinary object files have been searched. At least one of the files passed to dosld must be an ordinary object file unless the −u option is used (see −u above).

Files

/usr/bin/dosld

See Also

ar (CP), as (CP), cc (CP), ld (CP), ranlib (CP)

get (CP)   SOURCE CODE CONTROL SYSTEM   get (CP)

Name

get—generate ASCII text from an SCCS file

Synopsis

get [−r*SID*] [−c*cutoff*] [−i*list*] [−x*list*] [−a*sequence*] [−k] [−e] [−l[p]] [−p] [−m] [−n] [−s] [−b] [−g] [−t] filename . . .

Description

get creates an SCCS g-file (an ASCII text file) from each specified SCCS s-file. The name of each output g-file is derived by removing the beginning s.

from the corresponding input s-file name. For each file it processes, **get** reports (on standard output) the SID (SCCS Identification String) being processed and the number of lines that it retrieved from the SCCS s-file.

Identification Keywords

Identification information can be put into text retrieved from an SCCS file by substituting the value of $identification\ keywords$ for the $identification\ keywords$, described in Table 1-1. The %E% and %U% identification words described in the table can be used for nested gets.

Table 1.2 shows the allowable SCCS identification strings.

Options and Arguments

The arguments may be specified in any order. Each argument applies independently to each specified SCCS file.

$-asequence$ specifies the delta sequence number of the SCCS file delta to be retrieved. See $sccsfile$ (SCO 1988j) for additional details. The $-a$ option is used by the $comb$ (CP) command. If $-a$ is used together with $-e$, it may create an unexpected SID. However, if the $-a$ and $-e$ options are used with the $-r$ option, it can control the naming of the SID of the delta to be created. Only $-a$ is used if both $-a$ and $-r$ are specified.

$-b$ is used with the $-e$ option to specify that the new delta is to have an SID in a new branch (see Table 1-2). In order for this option to work, a b flag must be present in the s-file and the retrieved delta must be a leaf delta, i.e., a delta with no successors in the file tree.

Branch deltas can always be created from leaf deltas. Partial deltas are interpreted as shown in Table 1-2.

$-ccutoff$ specifies that no deltas applied after the cutoff date are to be included in the g-file (an ASCII text file described in the "Files" section below). The format of $cutoff$ is $YY[MM[DD[HH[MM[SS]]]]]$. Time or date units omitted from the cutoff specification default to their maximum value. For example, $-c9006$ defaults to $-c900628235959$. The individual 2-digit parts of the cutoff date may be separated by any number of non-numeric characters. This lets the user give a cutoff date in the following form: $-c90/06/01\ 12:00:00$.

$-e$ specifies that the new g-file to be created is to be editable. It causes a p-file to be created. Using the $-e$ option in a get for a given SID prevents additional $gets$ for the same SID until the $delta$ commmand is executed or unless the SCCS file gotten had a j (joint editing allowed) flag set by the $admin$ command. It is always possible for SCCS files with different SIDs to be edited concurrently.

TABLE 1-1.   Identification Keywords

Keyword	Value
%A%	Notation for creating what (CP) strings for non-XENIX system program files. %A% = %Z%%Y% %M% %I%%Z%
%B%	Delta branch number
%C%	Current line number for identifying messages
%D%	Current date (YY/MM/DD)
%E%	Creation date of the newest applied delta (YY/MM/DD)
%F%	SCCS filename
%G%	Creation date of the newest applied delta (MM/DD/YY)
%H%	Current date (MM/DD/YY)
%I%	*SID* (%R%.%L%.%B%.%S%) of the retrieved text
%L%	Delta level number
%M%	Module name (either the name of the SCCS file with s removed or, if the m flag is in the file, the value of the m flag)
%P%	SCCS filename (fully qualified)
%Q%	Value of the q flag in the SCCS file
%R%	Delta release number
%S%	Delta sequence number
%T%	Current time (HH:MM:SS)
%U%	Creation time of the newest applied delta (HH:MM:SS).
%W%	Notation for creating what (CP) strings for XENIX system program files. %W% = %Z%%M%<*horizontal-tab*>%I%
%Y%	Module type (value of the t flag in the SCCS file). See admin (CP)
%Z%	@(#), a four-character string recognized by what (CP)

If the −e option is specified, the *SID* of the delta to be created appears after the *SID* accessed but before the number of lines generated.

If the g-file created by using get −e is accidentally harmed during editing, get −k can re-create it. The −e option implies the −k option below.

The protection for SCCS files that is specified by the use of a ceiling, a floor, and a list of authorized users is in force when the −e option is used.

−g prevents actual retrieval of text from the SCCS file. This is used to verify the existence of a given *SID* or to create an l-file.

−i*list* specifies a *list* of new deltas to be included in the new g-file (see the "Files" section below). The *list* has syntax as follows:

```
<list> ::= <range> | <list> , <range>
<range> ::= SID | SID - SID
```

where *SID* may have the form shown in Table 1-2 above.

If the −i option is specified, any deltas included are listed following the notation "Included."

TABLE 1-2.   SCCS Identification Strings[10]

SID of Retrieved Delta	SID of Impending Delta	SID Specified[1]	Other Initial Conditions[2]
mR.mL	mR.(mL + 1)	None[3]	−b. R defaults to mR
mR.mL	mR.mL.(mB + 1).1	None[3]	no −b. R defaults to mR
mR.mL	R.1[4]	R	no −b. R > mR
mR.mL	mR.(mL + 1)	R	no −b. R = mR
mR.mL	mR.mL.(mB + 1).1	R	−b. R > mR
mR.mL	mR.mL.(mB + 1).1	R	−b. R = mR
hR.mL[5]	hR.mL.(mB + 1).1	R	n/r; R>mR; R nonexistent
R.mL	hR.mL.(mB + 1).1	R	n/r;[6]
R.L	R.(L + 1)	R.L	no -b.[7]
R.L	R.L.(mB + 1).1	R.L	−b[7]
R.L	R.L.(mB + 1).1	R.L	n/r;[8]
R.L.B.mS	R.L.B.(mS + 1)	R.L.B	no −b.[9]
R.L.B.mS	R.L.(mB + 1).1	R.L.B	−b.[9]
R.L.B.S	R.L.B.(S + 1)	R.L.B.S	no −b.[9]
R.L.B.S	R.L.(mB + 1).1	R.L.B.S	−b.[9]
R.L.B.S	R.L.(mB + 1).1	R.L.B.S	n/r. Branch successor

[1]R, L, B, and S specify the release, level, branch, and sequence parts of the SID, respectively, and m preceding such a part specifier stands for the maximum for that part. For example, "R.L.B.mS" means the maximum sequence number within release R, level L, and branch B. If any part R, L, B, or S of the SID is specified, then that part must exist.

[2]The −b option has an effect only if the b flag is present in the SCCS file. See admin (CP) for details. A table entry with "n/r" means that the −b option is irrelevant.

[3]No SID is specified if the d flag (default) is absent from the SCCS file. If d is present, however, the SID gotten from the d flag is treated as if it were specified on the command line.

[4]R.1 forces generation of the first delta in a new release.

[5]hR.mL is the highest release that exists and is lower than the specified nonexistent release R.

[6]The trunk successor in the release is greater than R, and R exists.

[7]No trunk successor.

[8]The trunk successor in the release is greater than or equal to R.

[9]No branch successor.

[10]Copyright ©1988 UNIX System Laboratories, Inc. All rights reserved. Reprinted with permission.

−k*list* prevents each identification keyword in the g-file from being expanded to its value. The −e option implies this option.

−l[p] causes an l-file (the delta summary) to be created. If lp is specified, the l-file is not created. Instead, the delta summary is written to standard output. See the "Files" section below.

−m causes each line of text retrieved from the SCCS file to be formatted as follows: SID of the delta that inserted the text line in the SCCS file, followed by a horizontal tab, followed by the line of text.

−n causes each line to be formatted as follows: %M% identification keyword, followed by a horizontal tab, followed by the line of text. If both −m and −n are used, the text line has the following format: %M% value, followed by a tab, followed by the format generated by −m.

−p writes the retrieved text to standard output without creating a g-file. Output normally sent to the standard output is sent to file descriptor 2 instead, unless it is thrown away by specifying the −s option.

−r*SID* uses *SID* to specify the version (delta) of the s-file to be retrieved by get. Table 1-2 above shows how *SID* specifies the version of the SCCS file retrieved. It also shows the *SID* of the version that later will be created later if the −e option is used.

−s suppresses output to standard output but not output to standard error.

−t accesses the most recently created delta in a specified release (e.g., −r2) or release and level (e.g., −r2.2.)

−x*list* specifies a *list* of deltas to be excluded from the new g-file. See −i above for *list* format.

If the −x option is used, any deltas excluded are listed following the notation "Excluded."

filename . . . specifies SCCS s-files input to get. If a directory is specified, get processes each file in the directory, except that non-SCCS files (the last part of the pathname does not begin with s) and unreadable files are ignored. If − specifies the filenames, each line from the standard input is taken to be the name of an SCCS file to be processed. Non-SCCS files and unreadable files are ignored in this case, too.

Files

The get (CP) command creates some auxiliary files, described below. The letter prepended before the hyphen is the file tag for these files. The name of each auxiliary file is formed by replacing the leading s of an s-file name by the appropriate file tag, except that the g-file name is derived simply by removing the s prefix. For example, with the s-file s.tuv.c, the g-file is tuv.c, while the l-file, p-file, and z-file are l.tuv.c, p.tuv.c, and z.tuv.c, respectively.

d-file is a temporary copy of the g-file, created during delta execution and deleted afterward.

g-file contains changes to be made to an original s-file. It exists before delta execution and is gone after delta execution is complete. The g-file is created whether or not the get generated any lines of text. It is created in the current directory if the −p option is not used. The g-file is owned by the real user. Only the real user needs write permission in the current directory. The mode of the g-file is 644 if the −k option is implied or used; otherwise, the mode is 444.

l-file has a table that tells which deltas were applied in creating the text retrieved by get. If the −l option is used, the l-file is created in the current

TABLE 1-3.   L-file table format

Line	Format
1. An asterisk (*) if the delta was not applied; otherwise, a blank	
2. A blank if the delta was applied or if it was not applied and was ignored; otherwise, an asterisk (*) if the delta was not applied and not ignored	
3. Reason the delta was or was not applied: "C" means cutoff (option −c), "I" means included, and "X" means excluded.	
4. Blank	
5. *SID*	
6. Tab character	
7. Date and time of creation (YY/MM/DD HH:MM:SS)	
8. Blank	
9. Login name of the delta creator	

directory. The mode of the l-file is 444. The l-file is owned by the user; only the real user needs write permission in the current directory. The format of the first few lines in the l-file table is as shown in Table 1-3. Comments and MR numbers follow on additional lines. Each entry is terminated by a blank line.

p-file contains the *SID* of the file being updated, the next *SID* when the g-file is restored to the s-file, and the *login* of the user retrieving the g-file. It exists before `delta` execution and may remain afterward. The p-file passes information to `delta` that is obtained if `get −e` is executed. The p-file contents prevent any additional executions of `get −e` until either `j`, the joint edit flag, is set in the SCCS file or `delta` is executed. See `admin` (CP) for additional details. The p-file has the following format: the *SID* of the gotten file, a blank, the *SID* of the impending delta, a blank, the login name of the real user, a blank, the date and time `get` was executed, a blank, and the `−i` option (if it was present), followed by a newline. There can be several lines in the p-file at once, but no two lines may have the same *SID* for an impending delta. The p-file is created in the same directory that contains the SCCS file. The effective user must have write permission in the directory. The mode of the directory is 644; it is owned by the effective user.

q-file is used by `delta` when it is updating a p-file. It is created during `delta` execution and deleted afterward.

`/usr/bin/bdiff` is a program to compute differences between g-file and the gotten file.

x-file is created whenever changes are made to an s-file. All actual changes are made to the x-file, holding the s-file safe in case of a crash. When changes are complete, the existing s-file is replaced by the x-file.

z-file is a lock file created to prevent simultaneous s-file updates by different users. It contains the binary process ID (2 bytes) of the currently executing SCCS process, i.e., get. The z-file is generated in the directory that contains the SCCS file during the get. The z-file has permission mode 444.

The effective user must have write permission in the directory. The mode of the directory is 644; it is owned by the effective user.

See Also

admin (CP), cdc (CP), comb (CP), delta (CP), get (CP), help (CP), prs (CP), rmdel (CP), sact (CP), sccsdiff (CP), unget (CP), val (CP), vc (CP), what (CP)

| gets (CP) | STRING INPUT | gets (CP) |

Name

gets—gets a string from stdout, the standard output.

Synopsis

gets [*string*]

Description

gets can be used together with csh (SCO 1988j), the shell command interpreter, to read a string from the standard input. gets then writes the string to standard output, or it writes a default *string* (see the *string* argument below) to standard output if an error occurs in reading the input string.

Options and Arguments

string specifies a default value to be used if an error occurs in reading from the standard input. If no *string* is specified, gets exits with an exit status of 1.

See Also

csh (SCO 1988j), line (SCO 1988j)

| hdr (CP) | XENIX COMPATIBILITY | hdr (CP) |

Name

hdr—display parts of a XENIX object file

Synopsis

hdr [-dhmprsSt] *filename* . . .

Description

hdr prints out seek positions for segments in object files, data or text relocation records (in ASCII), XENIX object file headers, and symbol tables. It
processes archives, a.out, x.out, and x.out segmented formats.

Symbol tables are printed in six fields:

- the symbol's position in the table, in decimal, starting with position zero,
- symbol type, in hexadecimal,
- s__seg field, in hexadecimal,
- hexadecimal value of the symbol,
- a character that represents the symbol type, and the
- symbol name.

The third field, s__seg, is omitted from a.out formats.

Short Form Relocation

The symbol format consists of three fields if short form relocation occurs.
The fields are

- relocation command, in hexadecimal,
- name of the referenced segment (text or data), and
- size of the relocation (short or long).

Long Form Relocation

The symbol format is six fields if long form relocation occurs. The fields are

- descriptor, in hexadecimal,
- symbol index or ID, in decimal,
- offset, in hexadecimal, within the current segment at which relocation takes
  place,
- name (bss, data, EXT for external, or text) of the segment referred to
  in the relocation,
- size of the relocation (byte, word, or long; a word is 2 bytes), and,
- if present, an indicator that relocation is relative.

The symbol index (second field) serves as an index to the symbol table during
external relocations, referring to an undefined symbol table entry.

Options and Arguments

−S displays file segment table and a header. The −S option is used only with x.out segmented relocation files.

−d displays data relocation records.

−h displays the object file header and the extended header with labeled fields—the default option.

−m displays data and text segments.

−p displays the symbol table.

−r displays both data and text relocation records.

−s displays the symbol table.

−t displays text relocation records.

filename . . . specifies object files created under XENIX.

See Also

nm (CP), a.out (SCO 1988j)

| help (CP) | SOURCE CODE CONTROL SYSTEM | help (CP) |

Name

help—get help about SCCS error messages and XENIX commands

Synopsis

help [*arg-type1*, or *arg-type2*, or *arg-type3*]

Description

help gets information that explains the use of a XENIX command, an SCCS command, or the error message displayed by an SCCS command. Type help stuck for information if you are stuck.

Options and Arguments

The help command will prompt for an argument if none is given. If an argument is given, it must be a message number (these normally appear in parentheses after messages) or a command name. The argument may be one of the following types:

arg-type1 is all numeric.

arg-type2 contains no numerics (command name such as delta).

arg-type3 starts with nonnumerics but ends with numerics. The nonnumeric prefix is an abbreviation for the command that generated the message. The numeric suffix designates one of a series of messages that may be produced by a particular SCCS command. For example, ge4 means message 4 from the get command.

Files

See the "Files" section of the entry for the get (CP) command for a description of all SCCS files.

/usr/lib/help is a directory that contains the text of SCCS help messages.

See Also

admin (CP), cdc (CP), comb (CP), delta (CP), get (CP), prs (CP), rmdel (CP), sact (CP), sccsdiff (CP), unget (CP), val (CP), vc (CP), what (CP)

---

ld (CP)	LINK EDITING	ld (CP)

Name

ld—link-edit common object files

Synopsis

ld [options] filename

Description

ld relocates code, resolves external references, and supports symbol tables for symbolic debugging. It combines object files (filename), in the specified order, into one executable object module, a.out. The a.out file is executable by default if no errors occurred during loading.

If ld does not recognize an input file as an object file, it assumes that the file is an archive file or a text file containing link editor directives. It assumes that files contain link editor directives if the files are not object or archive files. It then attempts to parse such files, sometimes warning about syntax errors.

If an argument specifies a library, the library is searched only once, at the point where it is encountered in the argument list. However, the ordering of library arguments is unimportant unless there is more than one library member that defines the same external symbol, because ld searches the library archive symbol table sequentially with as many passes as are required to resolve all of the external references that the library can satisfy. Space is saved by loading only those routines that resolve external references.

The reserved symbols, edata, etext, and end, are defined by the editor, so do not redefine them in a program. An additional limitation is that no arithmetic expression may have more than one forward-referenced symbol.

The library can be a relocatable archive or a shared library.

Options and Arguments

-L *dir* forces ld to search for libx.a in *dir* before searching in LIBDIR or LLIBDIR. This argument must precede the -l argument in order to work properly.

-M outputs a warning for each multiply defined external variable.

-N puts the data section immediately after the text section in the core image, and puts the text section at the start of the text segment instead of following all header information.

-V reports which version of ld is in use.

-VS *num* puts *num* (decimal) in the optional header of an a.out file as a stamp identifying the a.out version.

-Y[LU],dir changes the default directory for libraries.

L specifies that ld searches *dir* for libraries first, instead of in the first default library, LIBDIR.

U substitutes *dir* for LLIBDIR if ld has been prepared with LLIBDIR as a second default library and if U is specified. A warning is printed if U is specified when there is only one default directory.

-a generates an absolute file, the default option if option -r is not used. The -a option allocates memory for common symbols when it is used along with the -r option.

-e *esym* makes the address of *esym* the default entry point for the output file.

-f *fill* is a 2-byte constant that becomes the default fill pattern for holes within initialized bss sections, as well as within output sections.

-lx causes library libx.a to be searched (x is up to nine characters in length). The default libraries are LIBDIR or LLIBDIR. Placement of -lx in the list of options matters because a library is searched when its name is met.

-m generates a listing or map of the I/O section on standard output.

-o *outfile* generates an output object file, *outfile*. The default *outfile* is a.out.

-r preserves relocation entries in *outfile* so that *outfile* can be an input file in a future ld run. This way, ld will not warn about unresolved references and the output file will not be executable.

−s strips symbol table entries and line number information from *outfile*, the output object file.

−t suppresses warnings about multiply defined symbols with different sizes.

−u *symname* enters *symname* in the symbol table as an undefined symbol. This makes it easy to load routines entirely from the library because it supplies an unresolved reference needed to force loading of the first library routine. The −u *symname* option must be placed on the *ld* command line before the library that defines the symbol.

−x saves external and static symbols, but not local symbols, in the output symbol table, thereby saving space.

−z prohibits binding anything to virtual address zero so that null pointers can be detected at run time. C defines zero pointers as null pointers, and pointers which have zero assigned to them must not point at any object.

Files

a.out is the output file.
LIBDIR ordinarily is /lib.
LIBDIR/libx.a contains libraries.
LLIBDIR ordinarily is /usr/lib.
LLIBDIR/libx.a contains libraries.

See Also

as (CP), cc (CP), mkshlib (CP), a.out (SCO 1988j), ar (SCO 1988j), end (Peterson 1992), exit (Peterson 1992)

lex (CP)   LEXICAL/SYNTACTICAL ANALYSIS   lex (CP)

Name

lex—generate programs to do lexical analysis of text

Synopsis

lex [−rctvn] [*filename*] . . .

Description

lex generates programs (1) to divide input strings of characters into tokens which match specified patterns and (2) to execute routines in response to detecting

such tokens. The overall program created is yylex(). The library supplies a
main() which calls it.

The lex command creates a file, lex.yy.c. After compilation and loading
of libraries, lex.yy.c copies input to output, except if a specified pattern
is found in the input. In this case, the matching character string is stored in
yytext[], a character array. The number of characters in a matching
string is counted and stored in yyleng. Matching strings are left in yytext[].

Any string that starts with a blank is treated as C text and is copied. If such
a string precedes %%, it is copied to the definition section of lex.yy.c (see
below). Lines that start with a nonblank character and precede %% designate the
string on the left as the remainder of the line.

Input to lex consists of the lex source (the lex specification). The lex
specification has three sections: a definition section (optional), followed by a
rules section (mandatory), followed by a user subroutines section (optional).

Definition Section

The definition section may contain abbreviations, external definitions, #in-
clude statements, and #define statements. Abbreviations represent regular
expressions to be used in the rules section. These abbreviations simplify references to digits, letters, and blanks. Each abbreviation begins on the left end of
a line and, after one or more spaces, is followed by its definition. For example,
D [0-9] substitutes D for [0-9] in any references to [0-9] in the rules
or subroutines sections.

External definitions have the same purpose and form as in C. The special
#include file, y.tab.h, may contain #defines for token names.

The user may set table sizes (in the definitions section) for a finite state
machine, using the following definitions:

%a n sets the number of state transitions to n (default 2000).

%e n sets the number of parse tree nodes to n (default 1000).

%k n sets the number of of packed character classes to n (default 1000).

%n n sets the number of states to n (default 500).

%o n sets the size of the output array to n (default 3000).

%p n sets the number of positions to n (default 2500).

Using any of the above definitions implies using the −v option unless the
−n option is used instead (see the "Options and Arguments" section below).

Rules Section

The rules section begins with a %% delimiter. The section uses operators,
delimiters, and characters to describe patterns to be sought in the input and the
action to be taken when the specified pattern is found. The operators and delimiters have the following meanings:

[ ] means any single character from the string within the brackets. Ranges of alphabetic or numeric characters are designated using a hyphen, −. For example, [0−9] means any one of the 10 decimal digits.

{} is used as in the C language. The braces delimit an action extending over several lines of C code.

* means zero or more occurrences of the preceding expression.

+ means one or more occurrences of the preceding expression.

? means zero or one occurrence of the preceding expression, i.e., the preceding expression is optional.

. means any ASCII character except newline.

( ) is used for grouping.

| is used for separating alternatives. It has a lower precedence than *, ?, +, or concatenation.

reg{a,b} means between a and b occurrences of a regular expression, reg. It has a lower precedence than *, ?, +, or concatenation but a higher precedence than |.

^ preceding an expression lets the expression match a pattern only if a newline immediately precedes the expression.

$ is equivalent to \n. It indicates the end of a line, a special trailing context. For example, [ ]+$; causes all spaces at the end of a line to be ignored.

/ indicates trailing context. The part of the expression up to the slash (/) is sent to yytext, but the part of the expression following / must be present in the input stream.

" preceding and following an operator character allows its use as an ordinary character.

\ preceding an operator character allows its use as an ordinary character. For example, \ \ uses \ as an ordinary character, not as an escape character.

The rules section must end with a %% delimiter if a user subroutines section follows the rules section. If no %% is given, the rules section extends to the end of the program.

User Subroutines Section

Any user-defined routine may be put in the user subroutines section, but user-defined versions of input(), unput(c), and output(c) are particularly likely.

Three subroutines defined as macros are required: input() to read a character, unput(c) to replace a character in input after reading it, and output(c) to output a character.

The macros input() and output(c), use yyin to read from and yyout to write to, with stdin and stdout as default input and output, respectively.

Several functions allow sequences of characters to be treated in more than one way. The yymore( ) routine appends matching strings to those already in yytext[ ] instead of overwriting them. This facilitates handling a matching string that is a substring of another matching string. The yyless(n) function resets the endpoint of the matching string to the nth character of yytext[ ]. When the REJECT function appears on the right side of a rule, it causes a match to be rejected and the next suitable match to be executed instead.

Options and Arguments

−c causes C program actions in response to expressions.

−n suppresses the −v summary.

−r causes RATFOR program actions in response to expressions; it is not operational in System V Release 3.

−t writes lex.yy.c to standard output.

−v prints a one-line summary of statistics about input.

filename holds character strings and expressions to be analyzed and C source to be executed when specified expressions are detected. The default file is standard input. Multiple files are treated as a single file, and all files must be specified after any lex options are specified.

See Also

yacc (CP)

lint (CP)	DEBUGGING AIDS	lint (CP)

Name

lint—check C programs for bad features

Synopsis

lint [option] ... filenames ... library-descriptor(s)

Description

lint analyzes C program files, trying to find inconsistencies that may be bugs, unportable features, or features that waste resources. It detects automatic variables that are declared but not used, logical variables whose values do not change, loops entered elsewhere than at the top, and unreachable statements. It detects differences between the data type expected from a function and the data type actually returned. It also detects differences between the number of arguments (and/or their data type) expected by a function and the number of arguments (and/or their data type) actually received. It finds any functions whose returned values are not used and finds functions that return values at some places but not others.

The lint command cannot understand functions such as exit (Peterson 1992) or setjmp (Peterson 1992) that do not return.

The symbol "lint" should be regarded as a reserved word in code to be checked by lint because the preprocessor symbol "lint" is defined to permit code to be altered or removed before lint checking.

Lint Comments

Several C language comments in source code can change the behavior of lint. The comments are as follows:

/*ARGSUSED*/ activates the −v option for the next function.

/*LINTLIBRARY*/ acts like the −v and −x options. When placed at the beginning of a file, it suppresses warnings about unused functions and function arguments in the file.

/*NOTREACHED*/ suppresses warnings about code that is unreachable. This comment is useful when placed after calls to functions such as exit().

/*VARARGSn*/ prevents checking for variable numbers of arguments in the function it precedes. Data types of the first n arguments are checked. If n is missing, it is taken as 0.

Options and Arguments

When more than one option is used, they may be combined into a single argument, for example, −ab. The options may be used in any number, in any order, and filenames may be intermixed with options.

−D is the −D option of the preprocessor. See cpp (CP).

−I is the −I option of the preprocessor. See cpp (CP).

−O is the −O option of the compiler, recognized but ignored by lint. See cc (CP).

−U is the −U option of the preprocessor. See cpp (CP).

−a suppresses warnings about assignment of long variables to variables that are not long.

−b suppresses warnings about unreachable break statements.

−c produces a separate .ln file for each .c file specified on the command line. The list of .ln and llib-lx.ln files on the command line is ignored when −c is used. Only intrafile bugs are checked. This option suppresses any use of the $-o$ option. If the $-c$ option is not used, information from each separate source file is gathered and checked for consistency. The $-c$ option permits incremental use of lint on a set of source files, invoking lint with the $-c$ option once for each source file. After each source file has been separately processed by lint, the command is invoked again without the $-c$ option but with each .ln file listed, together with the necessary $-lx$ options. This lists any interfile inconsistencies. The $-c$ option permits make (CP) to restrict the action of lint to those files that have changed since the last time lint processed them.

$-g$ is the $-g$ option of the compiler, recognized but ignored by lint. See cc (CP).

$-h$ suppresses heuristic tests that try to find bugs, improve style, or reduce waste.

$-lx$ includes one more lint library, llib-lx.ln. For example, $-lm$ on the command line causes a lint version of the math library to be included.

$-n$ suppresses checks for compatibility with the standard or portable lint library.

$-o$ *libname* creates a lint library, llib-l*libname*.ln. See the $-c$ option above. The $-o$ option causes the input to the second pass of lint to be saved in the named library. Use the $-v$ option if the source files for the lint library are external references. Use the $-x$ option in order to create llibl*libname*.ln without producing warning messages about unused external variables. The effects of options $-v$ and $-x$ can be produced through the use of lint comments.

$-p$ enforces stricter checking. It tries to check portability to IBM and GCOS dialects of C. The option also truncates all nonexternal names to eight characters and all external names to six characters and one case. If $-p$ is used, lint appends the portable C lint library, llib-port.ln, to the end of the list of files on the command line instead of the default, llib-lc.ln.

$-u$ suppresses warnings about external variables and functions defined and not used or used and not defined.

$-v$ suppresses warnings about unused arguments of functions.

$-x$ suppresses warnings about variables referred to by external declarations but never used.

filenames are the files to be checked by lint. The filenames must end with .c for C source files or with .ln for files generated through an earlier use of lint with either the $-c$ or $-o$ option. Files with .ln extensions are analogous to object files (.o extensions) created by the compiler from input files with .c extensions. Files with other extensions cause warnings and are not processed.

library-descriptor(s) gives the names of libraries to use in checking the program.

Files

LLIBDIR ordinarily is /usr/lib, the directory where lint libraries required by the −lx option must be located.

LLIBDIR/lint[12] contains the first and second passes of lint.

LLIBDIR/llib-lc.ln contains C library function declarations (binary format; see LLIBDIR/llib-lc for source code).

LLIBDIR/llib-port.ln contains portable function delarations (binary format; see LLIBDIR/llib-port for source code).

LLIBDIR/llib-lm.ln contains math library function declarations (binary format; see LLIBDIR/llib-lm for source code).

TMPDIR ordinarily is /usr/tmp, but setting the environment variable TMPDIR can redefine it.

TMPDIR/*lint contains temporary files.

See Also

cc (CP), cpp (CP), make (CP)

---

lorder (CP)   LIBRARY MANAGEMENT   lorder (CP)

Name

lorder—finds an ordering relation for an object library

Synopsis

lorder *filenames* ...

Description

The lorder command lists pairs of object files or archive member names, showing which files depend on variables that are declared in other files. The first file of each pair refers to external variables that are defined in the second file.

The output from lorder may be sent to tsort (CP) to find a library ordering allowing one-pass access by ld (CP). Although this may make link-edit access somewhat more efficient, it is not required because the link editor, ld (CP), can make multiple passes over any archive that is in the portable archive format.

The following command sequence builds a new library, using existing .o files:

ar -cr *library* 'lorder *.o | tsort'

Options and Arguments

The lorder command has no options, but input files are specified on the command line as follows:

filenames is one or more object or archive files [compare with ar (CP)]. If there is more than one input file, any archive file or object suffix is acceptable. If there is only one input file, its suffix must be .o.

Files

TMPDIR/*symref contains temporary files.
TMPDIR/*symdef contains temporary files.
TMPDIR ordinarily is /usr/tmp, but it can be redefined by changing the environment variable TMPDIR. See tmpnam (Peterson 1992).

See Also

ar (CP), ld (CP), tsort (CP), ar (SCO 1988j), tmpnam (Peterson 1991)

m4 (CP)   PREPROCESSOR   m4 (CP)

Name

m4—macroprocessor

Synopsis

m4 [*options*] [*filenames*]

Description

m4 is a macroprocessor for RATFOR, C, and other computer languages. It processes argument files, *filenames*, in the order in which they are specified, writing the processed text to the standard output.

Macro names may consist of alphabetic characters, digits, and the underscore character, __. The first character may not be a digit.

Macro calls have the following form: name(*arg1*, *arg2*, . . . *argn*). No spaces may be between name and (, the leftmost parenthesis. If there is an intervening space, m4 assumes that the macro is being called without arguments.

When m4 collects arguments, it ignores leading unquoted blanks, tabs, and newlines. The value of any quoted string is the string, stripped of quotes. (See the built-in macro changequote below for a description of quote characters.)

When m4 recognizes a macro name, it collects the macro's arguments by searching for a right parenthesis. If fewer macro arguments are supplied than are specified by the macro definition, the trailing arguments are treated as null arguments. m4 continues evaluating macro arguments during the collection of arguments. The value of a macro is pushed back onto the input stream and rescanned after argument collection. Any commas or right parentheses encountered within the value of a nested call have the same effect as those within the original text.

Built-in Macros

Nearly three dozen built-in macros are available with the *m4* command. These may be redefined, but this causes the original meaning of such a macro to be forgotten. Macros have null values unless otherwise specified.

GET/OMIT Debugging Information

errprint( ) sends its arguments to the diagnostic output file.

dumpdef( ) prints names and definitions for specified items. All are printed if no arguments are specified.

traceon( ) turns on tracing for all macros if no arguments are specified. Otherwise, only the named macros are traced. A call to traceoff is required to untrace any macro specified by traceon.

traceoff( ) turns tracing off, both globally and for specified macros.

Manipulate Macro Arguments/Strings

changecom(*arg1*, *arg2*) disables comments if no arguments are specified. Otherwise, the left and right comment markers are changed from the default values of # and newline, respectively, if changecom has two arguments. If changecom has only one argument, the argument becomes the left marker and the right marker remains newline. Each comment marker may be up to five characters long.

changequote(*arg1*, *arg2*) changes argument quote symbols from the original values, ' ', to some other quote symbols, each up to five characters long. If no arguments are specified, the original quote symbols are restored.

decr(*arg*) returns the value of an argument after decrementing it by 1.

dnl( ) reads and discards the remaining characters of a line, including the newline.

eval(*expr*, *rad*, *dig*) has three arguments:

- an arithmetic expression,
- the radix for the result (octal or hex numbers may be specified as in C), and
- an argument specifying a minimum number of digits in the result.

The macro uses 32-bit arithmetic to evaluate the expression. Expressions may contain arithmetic operators: %, +, −, *, /, ˆ (exponentiation); bitwise operators: &, |, ˆ , and ˜; relational operators; and parentheses.

ifelse(*string1*, *string2*, *string3* . . .) permits conditional testing of its arguments. If *string1* is identical to *string2*, then the value of ifelse is *string3*. Otherwise, if there are five or more arguments, testing is repeated with arguments 4, 5, 6, and 7. But if *string1* and *string2* are not identical and no fourth string is present, the macro value is null.

incr(*arg*) interprets its initial digit-string argument as a decimal number, increments it by 1, and returns that value.

index(*string1*, *string2*) returns the position in *string1* where *string2* starts (zero origin is assumed). If *string2* is not present, the macro returns − 1.

len(*arg*) returns the character length of its argument.

shift(*arg1*, *arg2*, . . . *argn*) returns all its arguments except the first. These arguments are quoted, have commas inserted between them, and are pushed back. The quotes nullify the effect of an extra scan that will be performed later.

substr(*string*, *start*, *length*) returns a substring of *string* which begins at *start* and is *length* long. If the third argument is missing, the substring is taken to be large enough to extend to the end of the first string.

translit(*string*, *char*, *replace*) replaces each character in *string* which matches a character in *char* with the corresponding character in *replace*. For example, translit(cat, cats, DOGS) returns DOG.

Manipulate Macro Definitions

define(*name*, *substitution*) has the following arguments: The first macro argument, argument 0, is the macro name. The second argument of define becomes the value of the macro whose name is the first argument.

Each instance of $*n* in the replacement text is replaced by the *n*th argument; *n* is an integer. $# is replaced by the number of macro arguments. $* is replaced by a comma-separated list of arguments. $@ is replaced by a comma-separated list of arguments; each argument is quoted. Missing arguments are replaced by nulls.

defn(*arg1*, *arg2*, . . .) can rename macros. It returns the quoted definition of its argument(s).

ifdef(*arg1*, *arg2*, *arg3*) returns a value equal to *arg2* if *arg1* is defined; otherwise, it returns *arg3*. The value is null if there is no *arg3*. The predefined word XENIX can be used with *m4*.

popdef(arg1, arg2, . . .) deletes the current definition of its arguments. This brings the previous definition, if any, into view.

pushdef(*arg1*, *arg2*, . . .) works like define() but also saves the previous definition.

undefine() deletes the definition of the macro specified in its argument.

Manipulate Streams

divert(*digit-string*) diverts the current output stream to the stream specified by *digit-string* (m4 has up to 10 output streams, numbered 0-9). Final output consists of the concatenation of streams in numeric order. Output diverted to streams other than streams 0-9 is thrown away.

divnum() returns the value of the current stream (usually, it is 0–9; see divert above).

undivert() immediately outputs text from diversions specified by arguments, or from all diversions if none is specified. Undiverting throws the diverted text away. Text can be undiverted to another diversion.

Manipulate Process Environment

include(*file*) returns the contents of *file*.

maketmp() puts the ID of the current process in string *XXXXX* in the macro's arguments.

m4exit() causes exit from m4. The exit code is argument 1, if specified. Otherwise, it is 0.

m4wrap() pushes argument 1 back at final EOF.

sinclude() is the same as include, except that m4 silently continues processing if a specified file cannot be found.

syscmd() executes the XENIX system command specified by the macro's first argument. For example, syscmd(date) executes the date command and includes it in m4 output. No value is returned.

sysval() gives the return code from the most recent execution of syscmd.

Options and Arguments

−B*int* sets the size of the argument-collection and pushback buffers to some other value than the default (4096).

−D*name*[= *val*] defines the value of *name* to be *val* if *val* is specified. Otherwise, *name* is null. If the −D flag is used, it must appear after any filenames or other flags (other than −U).

−H*int* sets the size of the symbol table hash array to *int*, a prime value (default is 199).

−S*int* sets the size of the call stack to *int* (default is 100). Macros require three slots. Nonmacro arguments require one.

−T*int* sets the size of the token buffer to *int* (default is 512).

−U*name* causes *name* to be undefined. If the −U flag is used, it must appear after any filenames or other flags (other than −D).

−e specifies interactive operation with unbuffered output. Interrupts are ignored.

−s enables line sync output for *cpp*, i.e., *#line* . . .

filenames specifies input files. Input comes from the standard input if no file is specified or if *filenames* is −.

See Also

cc (CP), cpp (CP)

---

make (CP)   **VERSION CONTROL**   **make (CP)**

Name

make—maintain, update, or regenerate program groups

Synopsis

make [−f *makefile*] [−p] [−i] [−k] [−s] [−r] [−n] [−b] [−e] [−t] [−q] [−d] [*names*]

Description

make automates the creation, maintenance, and updating of groups of programs. It uses several kinds of information: a description file supplied by the user, filenames, dates when files were last modified, and built-in rules. Using these elements, make executes commands specified in *makefile* in order to update target files selectively. Any target file is updated only if its dependents are newer than it is. Any prerequisite files (dependencies) of a target are recursively added to the list of targets. Missing files are treated as being outdated.

Description Files

makefiles typically contain a series of entries specifying dependencies. The first line of each entry is a blank-separated, nonnull list of target files, followed by a colon (:), then by a list of prerequisite files or dependencies (may be a null list). If `include` comprises the first seven letters of a line in *make-file*, and is followed by a blank or tab, the remainder of the line is treated as a filename and is read after substitution of any macros. Any text following a semicolon (;) and any following lines that start with a tab are shell commands that need to be executed to update the target file. Shell commands can extend from a first line to a second line if a backslash (\) and a newline mark the end of the first line. For example, the sequence

```
echo s\
db
```

will display `sdb`. Commands that the shell executes directly, for example, `cd` (CP), will not work across newlines in `make`.

Any nonempty line starting with a character other than a sharp (#) or tab begins a new macro definition or dependency. A *makefile* can have comments. These are delimited by sharp (#) and newline.

Macros

The *makefile* may contain user-defined macros, defined by entries having the form *string1* = *string2*. Subsequent occurrences of *string1* in $(*macro*[:*string1*=[*string2*]]) are replaced by *string2*. Parentheses are required if the macro name is not a single character. Strings in such substitutions are delimited by blanks, newline characters, tabs, or beginnings of lines. *string2* consists of all characters up to an unescaped newline or comment character. Nonoverlapping occurrences of *string1* are replaced by *string2*.

Makefile Example

The following example illustrates a simple `makefile` in which a target program, `prog`, depends on three object files—`x.o`, `y.o`, and `z.o`—which are, in turn, dependent on their source files—`x.c`, `y.c`, and `z.c`—and on an include file used by all three, `incl.h`:

```
#comments here
prog: x.o y.o z.o
    cc x.o y.o z.o -o prog
x.o: inc.h x.c
    cc -c x.c
y.o: incl.h y.c
    cc -c y.c
z.o: incl.h z.c
    cc -c z.c
```

Internal Macros

Internally maintained macros are useful for writing rules for generating targets. These are the available built-in macros:

$%$ expands to the name of a library member. It is evaluated only when the target is an archive library member like `lib(file.o)`. Here, $@$ evaluates to `lib`, while $%$ evaluates to `file.o`.

$*$ expands to the filename part of the current dependent, but without the suffix. It is evaluated only for inference rules.

$<$ expands to the filename of the first dependent that is younger than the target. It is evaluated only for inference rules or for the `.DEFAULT` rule (see `.DEFAULT` below).

$?$ is evaluated when explicit rules from *makefile* are evaluated. It expands to the string of filenames of all dependents that are younger than the current target, i.e., a string of names of files that need to be rebuilt because they are out of date with respect to the target.

$@$ expands to the complete pathname of the current target. It is evaluated only for explicitly named dependencies.

If D is appended to $%$, $*$, $<$, or $@$, i.e., if they become $(\%D)$, $(*D)$, $<$, or $(@D)$, the macro expansion is to the directory part of the target name. If F is appended to any of these four macros, the expansion is to the file part of the name. If no directory part exists, `./` is generated.

Environment Variables

`make` reads the environment and processes any environment variables as macros. It interacts with the environment through a macro, MAKEFLAGS, that is maintained by `make`. MAKEFLAGS is defined as all the input flag arguments collected together into a string (but without minus signs). MAKEFLAGS is exported, so it is usable by further invocations of `make`. Any command line assignments and flags update the string in MAKEFILE. The MAKEFLAGS environment variable, as processed by `make`, may contain any legal option except $-f$, $-p$, or $-r$ defined for the command line. If a variable is not in the environment, `make` puts the current options in it and passes MAKEFLAGS on to the invocations of commands, so that MAKEFLAGS always holds the current input options. Thus, if $-n$ is put in MAKEFLAGS, `make` $-n$ can be performed recursively on an entire software system to see what would happen if the system had actually been executed because $-n$ is passed to subsequent invocations of $(MAKE)$.

Upon execution, `make` assigns macro definitions in the following order of precedence:

1. `make` reads the internal list of macro definitions.

2. **make** reads the environment, treating environment variables as macro definitions and marking them as exported.
3. **make** reads **makefile**(s). Assignments found in **makefile**(s) override the environment. What the user sees is what the user gets, unless the −e command line flag is used to tell **make** that the environment overrides the assignments in **makefile**(s). Suffixes (see the "Suffixes" section below) and their associated rules in **makefile**(s) override any suffixes in built-in rules (see the following section).

Inference Rules

make has a set of internal rules for building files. Some files obviously depend on other files. For example, files with .o (object) suffixes depend on other files with suffixes such as .s (assembly source) or .c (C language source). The rule for creating a file with an .o suffix from a file with an .s suffix is specified by an entry that has .c.o: as the target and no dependents. Shell commands that are associated with the target define the rule for creating a file with an .o suffix from a file with an .s suffix.

In the absence of an explicit update command in a *makefile*, make may still cause a dependent file to be compiled in order to build a specified target because **make** infers that the compilation is required. The source file **rules.c** contains internal rules governing such activity. You may modify these rules or add rules to the list simply by adding them to **makefile**.

In order to print out the rules in a form acceptable for recompilation, execute the following command:

```
make −fp − 2>/dev/null </dev/null
```

printf, used to print the output from the above command, prints (null) when it is handed a null string.

Suffixes

The list of filename suffixes that *make* recognizes is given in Table 1-4. The list is the dependency list for the name .SUFFIXES. The order of the list is significant because the list is scanned from left to right. The first name for which both a rule and a file exist is regarded as a prerequisite. If .SUFFIXES is given without dependencies, it clears the dependency list. To print out the suffixes, execute make −fp − 2>/dev/null </dev/null.

Some suffixes require tildes because **make**'s treatment of suffixes is incompatible with SCCS's use of .s prefixes. The tilde converts a file reference into an SCCS file reference.

Table 1-5 below shows the predefined macros that **make** recognizes. These macros specify some substitutions in inference rules. For example, the default

TABLE 1-4.   Dependency list for .SUFFIXES

Suffix	File
.o	Object file
.c	C Source file
.s	Assembler source file
.y	yacc source file
.l	lex source file

inference rules may use the following macros to support inclusion of certain options in commands:

- CFLAGS is used for compiler options to cc (CP),
- LFAGS is used for compiler options to lex (CP),
- YFLAGS is used for compiler options to yacc (CP).

Table 1-6 shows six default single-suffix rules that make uses. Single-suffix rules tell how to build *y* from *y*.c. These rules are used for building targets from only one dependent file.

Finally, in addition to recognizing .c.c˜, .f.f˜, and .sh.sh˜ [see sccsfile (SCO 1988j)], make recognizes the other double-suffix rules shown in Table 1-7.

Command Lines

Each command line is executed by its own shell. Command lines are executed one at a time.

TABLE 1-5.   Some pre-defined macros recognized by make

```
AR = ar
ARFLAGS = -rv
AS = as
ASFLAGS =
CC = cc
CFLAGS = -o
GET = get
GFLAGS =
LD = ld
LDFLAGS =
LEX = lex
LFLAGS =
MAKE = make
YACC = yacc
YFLAGS =
```

TABLE 1-6.   Single-suffix rules that govern *make*

Suffix	Action
.c:	$(CC) $(CFLAGS) $(LDFLAGS) $< -o $@
.c˜ :	$(GET) $(GFLAGS) $<
	$(CC) $(CFLAGS) $(LDFLAGS) $*.c -o $*
	-rm -f $*.c
.sh:	cp $< $@; chmod 0777 $@
.sh˜ :	$(GET) $(GFLAGS) $<
	cp $*.sh $*; chmod 0777 $@
	-rm -f $*.sh

.DEFAULT causes commands associated with the name .DEFAULT (if it exists) to be used if a file is to be created but there are no explicit commands or relevant built-in rules.

.IGNORE has the same effect on command line execution as the -i option. It causes make to continue executing if a command returns nonzero (error) status; ordinarily, make would terminate if a command returned error status. Also, if a line that specifies a command begins with a tab followed by a hyphen, *make* ignores command error status and continues executing.

.PRECIOUS retains dependents of a target even if Interrupt or Quit is pressed.

.SILENT has the same effect as the -s option. Each command line is printed when it is executed unless the entry .SILENT is in *makefile* or the -s option is used (see -s below).

Libraries

Any dependency or target name containing parentheses is treated as the name of an archive library. Any string within the parentheses refers to a library member. If the LIB macro is defined, $(LIB)(file.o) or lib(file.o) designates a library with file.o as a member. The expression (lib(filea.o fileb.o filec.o) is not legal.

Rules for archive libraries look like .YY.a. The archive member name is made from the suffix YY. It is impossible to build lib(filea.o) from filea.o because the YY must be different from the suffix of the archive member.

Options and Arguments

Options are specified on the command line. Command lines are executed one by one. Each is executed by its own shell. The default shell is /bin/sh.

Command arguments are evaluated as follows: First, macros (arguments hav-

TABLE 1-7.   Double-suffix rules that govern make

Suffix	Action

.c˜c, .s˜s, .sh˜sh, .y˜y, .l˜l, .h˜h
Any of the preceding seven pairs of suffixes causes the following action:

```
                    $(GET) $(GFLAGS) $<
.c.a:               $(CC) -c $(CFLAGS) $<
                    $(AR) $(ARFLAGS) $@ $*.o
                    rm -f $*.o
.c˜ .a:             $(GET) $(GFLAGS) $<
                    $(CC) -c $(CFLAGS) $*.c
                    $(AR) $(ARFLAGS) $@ $*.o
                    rm -f $*.[co]
.c.o:               $(CC) $(CFLAGS) -c $<
```

The following rule transforms an SCCS C source file into an object file:

```
.c˜ .o:             $(GET) $(GFLAGS) $<
                    $(CC) $(CFLAGS) -c $*.c
                    -rm -f $*.c
.s˜ .a:             $(GET) $(GFLAGS) $<
                    $(AS) $(ASFLAG) -o $*.o $*.s
                    $(AR) $(ARFLAGS) $@ $*.o
                    -rm -f $*.[so]
.s.o:               $(AS) $(ASFLAG) -o $@ $<
.s˜ .o:             $(GET) $(GFLAGS) $<
                    $(AS) $(ASFLAG) -o $*.o $*.s
                    -rm -f $*.s
.l.c:               $(LEX) $(LFLAGS) $<
                    mv lex.yy.c $@
.l.o:               $(LEX) $(LFLAGS) $<
                    $(CC) $(CFLAGS) -c lex.yy.c
                    rm lex.yy.c
                    mv lex.yy.o $@
                    -rm -f $*.l
.l˜ .o:             $(GET) $(GFLAGS) $<
                    $(LEX) $(LFLAGS) $*.l
                    $(CC) $(CFLAGS) -c lex.yy.c
                    rm -f lex.yy.c $*.l
                    mv lex.yy.o $*.o
.y.c:               $(YACC) $(YFLAGS) $<
                    mv y.tab.c $@
.y˜ .c:             $(GET) $(GFLAGS) $<
                    $(YACC) $(YFLAGS) $*.y
                    mv y.tab.c $*.c
                    -rm -f $*.y
.y.o:               $(YACC) $(YFLAGS) $<
                    $(CC) $(CFLAGS) -c y.tab.c
                    rm y.tab.c
                    mv y.tab.o $@
.y˜ .o:             $(GET) $(GFLAGS) $<
                    $(YACC) $(YFLAGS) $*.y
                    $(CC) $(CFLAGS) -c y.tab.c
                    -rm -f y.tab.c $*.y
                    mv y.tab.o $*.o
```

ing equals signs embedded) are examined and all assignments are made. Second, make examines option arguments. Finally, make assumes that any remaining arguments are the names of targets, and it processes the arguments from left to right.

The first name in the description file that starts with a character other than a period is taken to be a target if make finds no target arguments on the command line.

−b allows makefiles written for the old version of make to run without errors. This version of *make* requires all dependency lines to have a command associated with them (the command may be null). The previous version of make assumed that the command was null if no command was explicitly specified.

−d prints out information about files. This is the debug mode.

−e causes environment variables to override macro assignments in a makefile.

−f *makefile* specifies the description file. More than one −f *makefile* argument may be specified. If a filename of − is used, it specifies the standard input file as the description file. If −f has no arguments, make searches for the description in the current directory, in the following files, and in the following order: makefile, Makefile, s.makefile, and s.Makefile. If description files are present, their contents override built-in rules. This option cannot be specified in the MAKEFLAGS environment variable.

−i causes make to ignore error codes returned by commands invoked by make. Otherwise, such errors stop make. If the description file contains the fake target name .IGNORE, make enters this mode. Some commands wrongly return a nonzero status; use −i to overcome this problem.

−k stops processing the current entry if it fails but continues processing other branches that do not depend on the current entry.

−n prints commands but does not execute them (nonexecute mode). However, lines starting with @ are printed. Also, a command line is always executed if it contains the string $(MAKE). Thus, make −n can be executed recursively on an entire software system because −n is put in the MAKEFLAGS environment variable and passed to subsequent invocations of $(MAKE), allowing make-file debugging without actual execution.

−p prints all macro definitions and target descriptions (dependency lines) in the makefile. This option cannot be specified in the MAKEFLAGS environment variable.

−q causes make to return a status code of zero if a target file is up-to-date, and nonzero if it is not.

−r suppresses the use of built-in rules for transforming a file with one suffix to a file with another suffix.

−s stops command lines from being printed before execution (silent mode). If the description file contains the fake target name .SILENT, make enters this mode.

−t touches target files, updating the modification dates of a file without changing the file or executing commands.

names is ordinarily the name of a program. The *names* cannot have the following characters: =, :, or @.

Files

[Mm]akefile
s.[Mm]akefile

See Also

cc (CP), lex (CP), yacc (CP), printf (Peterson 1991), sccsfile (SCO 1988j), cd (SCO 1988j), sh (SCO 1988j)

masm (CP)	ASSEMBLY	masm (CP)

Name

masm—invoke the assembler

Synopsis

masm [*options*] *sourcefile*

Description

masm is the 8086/80286/80386 assembler. The assembler reads 8086/80286/ 80386 assembly language instructions from *sourcefile* and creates a linkable object file named *sourcefile*.o or an executable program, a.out.

Options and Arguments

−C outputs cross-reference information about a set of files to files that have the same names as the input files but filename extensions of '.erf.' The default setting of −C is false; no cross-reference data are output.

−D*sym* defines the symbol *sym* as a null TEXTMACRO. The default setting of the −D flag is NULL; *sym* has no meaning if it is not defined.

−I*path* defines *path* as the search path for include files. One invocation of masm may have up to 10 include files. The default setting of the −I flag is NULL; *path* has no meaning if it is not defined.

−Ml causes the case of symbols to be let alone. This is the default condition for the −M option. See -Mx and -Mu below.

−Mu causes upper case to be treated as identical to lower case.

−Mx causes masm to preserve lowercase letters in public and external names only when it is copying these to the object file. Otherwise, masm converts lowercase to uppercase.

−Oobjfile copies the assembled instructions (in binary) to objfile. The default value of the −O flag is FALSE, meaning that output will be in binary.

−X copies to the assembly listing any statements that form the body of an IF directive even though the condition of the IF directive evaluates as false. The default value of the −X flag is *FALSE*, meaning that statements forming the body of an IF directive will not be copied if the condition evaluates to false.

−a puts the assembled output segments in alphabetic order before they are copied to the object file. The −a option is a flag whose default setting is FALSE, i.e., segments will not be output in alphabetic order.

−cfilename.crf outputs cross-reference information to filename.crf. The default for the −c flag is FALSE, meaning that no cross-reference data are output.

−dfilename adds a listing from pass 1 to the assembly listing file, filename.1st. The default value of −d is FALSE; pass 1 is not added to filename.1st.

−e generates floating point code that emulates an 8087 or 80287 numeric coprocessor. It is necessary to link programs created with this option to an appropriate math library before they are executed. The default setting of the −e flag is FALSE, meaning that there will be no floating point emulation.

−llistfile creates an assembly listing file that has the same basename as sourcefile or that has the name listfile.1st if listfile is specified. The file lists (for each instruction) the source instructions, assembled code (binary), and any assembly errors detected. If listfile is '−,' the listing is sent to stdout. The default value of listfile is sourcefile.1st.

−n generates symbol information. This option must be used with the −l option. The default value of the −n flag is TRUE, meaning that symbols will be output if −l is used.

−oobjfile copies the assembled instructions (in octal) to objfile. objfile is executable only if assembly was error-free. The objfile filename overrides the default object filename. The default value of the −o flag is TRUE, meaning that the assembled output will be in binary.

−r generates floating point code that requires an 8087 or 80287 math coprocessor for execution. The default value of the −r flag is TRUE, meaning that there will be real instead of emulated floating point computation.

-v causes verbose error statistics to be printed on the console. Otherwise, only error counts are displayed. The default value of the **-v** flag is FALSE, meaning that only error counts will be displayed.

-x displays error messages on standard error output in addition to the messages in the listing file. The default value of the **-x** flag is TRUE, meaning that errors will be displayed on the console.

sourcefile contains 8086/80286/80386 assembly language to be assembled. The assembler will display a warning if *sourcefile* lacks an .s extension, but the extension is not required.

Files

/bin/masm

See Also

cc (CP), ld (CP), a.out (SCO 1988j)
XENIX System V Development System: Macro Assembler User's Guide (SCO 1988e)

Return Value

The masm command returns exit codes having the following meaning:

Exit Code	Code Meaning
0	no errors
1	argument error
2	can't open input file
3	can't open listing file
4	can't open object file
5	can't open cross-reference file
6	can't open include file
7	assembly errors; the object file is deleted if the errors are fatal
8	error in allocating memory
9	this version allows no real number input

mkstr (CP)	C STRING MANIPULATION	mkstr (CP)

Name

mkstr—create an error message file from C source

Synopsis

mkstr [-] *message-file prefix-file*

Description

mkstr creates files of error messages. The utility processes each specified file, putting a modified version of the input file in a specified output file (*prefix-file*). The utility can shrink the size of programs that have large numbers of error diagnostics, thereby reducing system overhead, since error messages no longer have to be swapped in and out as often.

A sample mkstr command line is as follows:

mkstr *estrings prefix-filename*

which takes error messages from C source files in the current directory, places them in the file *estrings* and puts processed copies of the error messages in the file *prefix-filename*.

The mkstr command looks for the string 'error('' in the input stream. Each time it finds this token, it puts the C string following the ''' into the message file, followed by a null character and a newline character. The purpose of the null character is to terminate the message so that it may be more easily used when retrieved. The newline is used to *cat* the message file to review its contents. The processed copy of the input file contains an *lseek* pointer that may be used to retrieve the messages.

The mkstr command changes

error("Unable to find error msg", *arg1, arg2, arg3*);

into

error(*pos*, *arg1, arg2, arg3*);

where *pos* is the seek position of the string in the processed error message file.

It is up to the programmer to create a routine that opens the message file, reads the string, and prints it.

Options and Arguments

– causes error messages to be put at the end of the specified message file for recompiling a portion of a large mkstred program.

message-file contains error messages. This is the only necessary argument.

prefix-file is the output filename formed by putting the specified *prefix* in front of the original file name.

See Also

xstr (CP), lseek (Peterson 1991)

---

nm (CP)	OBJECT FILE MANIPULATION	nm (CP)

Name

nm—display a symbol table of common object file(s)

Synopsis

nm [-acgnoOprsSuV] [+*offset*][*filename* . . .]

Description

nm prints the symbol table (name list) of each common object file, *filename*, given in the argument list. The common object file(s) may be archive(s) of relocatable or absolute common object file(s), or they may be relocatable or absolute common object files. nm processes both XENIX-generated object files and COFF files. It translates COFF symbols into standard XENIX object symbols whenever possible.

Output Format

Each defined symbol name is displayed following its value (hexadecimal) and one of the following type letters:

- A (absolute symbol),
- B (bss segment),
- C (common symbol),
- D (data segment symbol),
- K (8086 common segment),
- S (user-defined segment symbol),
- T (text segment symbol), or
- U (undefined).

If the symbol being displayed is local, the type letter is displayed in lowercase. If the symbol table is in segmented format (see option −S), nm displays symbol values as `segment:offset`. Output is sorted alphabetically by default (see option −n).

Options and Arguments

The following options may be used singly or in combination, in any order. They may appear anywhere on the command line.

−O prints symbol values (octal).

−S toggles the display format between segmented format and nonsegmented format. Executable files and object files for 80386 systems have segment offsets that are 32 bits rather than 16 bits long.

−a tries to print the symbol table of every module in an archive library. This option causes nm to report any library members that are not valid object modules instead of silently ignoring such modules. The −a option will always generate at least one error message when used on a library that has been processed by `ranlib` (CP) because `ranlib` produces, as the first member of the library, a module, __.SYMDEF that is not a valid object module.

−c prints only C program symbols (symbols whose names begin with an underscore, '_').

−g prints only external (global) symbols.

−n sorts output numerically (default is alphabetic).

−o prepends a file or archive element name (as appropriate) to each line of output instead of once per file or archive element.

−p prints output in symbol table order without sorting.

−r sorts output in reverse order.

−s sorts on symbol size instead of on value; it displays the symbol's size. This option implies the use of the −n option. The last symbol in each data or text segment can be assigned size 0.

filename specifies the file whose symbol table is to be listed. The default file is `a.out`.

See Also

`as` (CP), `cc` (CP), `ld` (CP), `a.out` (SCO 1988j), `ar` (SCO 1988j), `tmpnam` (Peterson 1992)

prof (CP)	PROFILING	prof (CP)

Name

`prof`—display profile data produced by the *monitor* function

Synopsis

prof [-a] [-l] [*filename*]

Description

prof creates a report that shows the amount of execution time spent in different parts of a program and the number of times each function is called. It does this by interpreting a file, mon.out, generated by the monitor (Peterson 1992) system routine.

In order to profile a program, the program must first be compiled using the -p (profile) option of cc (CP), the compiler. This adds code to each subroutine to count the number of times it is called. Code is inserted that generates calls to monitor. Later, when the program is executed, monitor watches program execution and automatically creates mon.out, containing subroutine execution counts that prof subsequently interprets. (It is best to run a program immediately before profiling it to avoid using an old mon.out file by mistake.)

The -p option of cc causes calls to monitor to be inserted at the beginning and end of execution of programs that call exit (CP) or that return from main. Other programs require that a final call to monitor be coded explicitly.

The symbol table in the object file *filename* (the default is a.out) is correlated with the profile file, mon.out. For each external symbol in the program, prof calculates the percentage of execution time spent executing between that external symbol and the next. The symbols are listed in decreasing order of the amount of execution time. prof also lists the number of times each routine was called and the number of milliseconds consumed by each call.

Although prof makes a precise count of the number of function calls, the times reported in successive runs may vary by more than 20 percent. Hidden background processes or asynchronous processes, as well as normal processes, may cause a varying cache hit rate because the program being profiled is sharing the cache with these other processes.

Options and Arguments

-a causes all symbols to be reported, not just external symbols.
-l lists output by symbol value instead of by decreasing percentage of time.
filename is the object file whose symbol table is to be displayed.

Files

a.out contains the symbol table (namelist).
mon.out contains profile data.

See Also

cc (CP), exit (CP), prof (CP), profil (CP), monitor (Peterson 1992)

---

prs (CP)	SOURCE CODE CONTROL SYSTEM	prs (CP)

Name

prs—print an SCCS file

Synopsis

prs [−d[*dataspec*]] [−r[*SID*]] [−e] [−l] [−a] *filenames*

Description

prs is one of a group of 14 commands used to keep track of files as they evolve through various versions. It prints all or part of one or more .s-files (SCCS files) on the standard output in a format supplied by the user.

Data Keywords

The data keywords below specify which parts of an .s-file should be retrieved and printed. Every part of an SCCS file has a data keyword associated with it. Any data keyword may appear in *dataspec* an unlimited number of times. The prs command prints user-supplied text and values extracted from the SCCS file and substituted for data keywords in their order of appearance in *dataspec*. User-supplied text is text other than a data keyword.

Any data keyword value has either a simple (s) format, in which keywords are directly substituted, or a multiline (m) format, in which a carriage return follows each substitution. Each tab is specified by \t and each carriage return/ newline pair is specified by \n.

Table 1-8 shows the default data keywords in the delta table section of a file.

The default data keywords in the "User Names" section of the file are as follows:

Keyword	Data Item	Format	Value
:UN:	names of users	m	text

Table 1-9 shows the default data keywords in the flags section of the file.

TABLE 1-8.   Default data keywords in delta table section of file

Keyword	Data Item	Format	Value
:Dt:	Delta information	s	See note 1
:DL:	Delta line statistics	s	:Li:/:Ld:/:Lu:
:Li:	Lines inserted	s	$nnnnn$
:Ld:	Lines deleted	s	$nnnnn$
:Lu:	Lines not changed	s	$nnnnn$
:DT:	Delta type	s	D~ or R~
:I:	SCCS ID string	s	:R:.:L:.:B:.:S:
:R:	Release number	s	$nnnn$
:L:	Level number	s	$nnnn$
:B:	Branch number	s	$nnnn$
:S:	Sequence number	s	nnnn
:D:	*Date delta made*	*s*	:Dy:/:Dm:/:Dd:
:Dy:	Year delta made	s	nn
:Dm:	Month delta made	s	nn
:Dd:	Day delta made	s	nn
:T:	Time delta made	s	:Th:::Tm:::Ts:
:Th:	Hour delta made	s	nn
:Tm:	Minutes delta made	s	nn
:Ts:	Seconds delta made	s	nn
:P:	Programmer ID	s	*logname*
:DS:	Delta sequence number	s	$nnnn$
:DP:	Seq.-no. of preceding delta	s	$nnnn$
:DI:	Seq.-no. deltas ignore, excl., inc.	s	:Dn:/:Dx:/:Dg:
:Dn:	Seq.-no. of included deltas	s	:DS:~ :DS:...
:Dx:	Seq.-no. of excluded deltas	s	:DS:~ :DS:...
:Dg:	Seq.-no. of ignored deltas	s	:DS:~ :DS:...
:MR:	MR numbers of a delta	m	*text*
:C:	Comments for delta	m	*text*

Note 1: :Dt:~ =~ :DT:~ :I:~ :D:~ :T:~ :P:~ :DS:~ :DP:

The default data keywords in the "Comments" section of the file are as follows:

Keyword	Data Item	Format	Value
:FD:	file description	m	text

The default data keywords in the "Body" section of the file are as follows:

Keyword	Data Item	Format	Value
:BD:	body	m	text
:GB:	body gotten	m	text

Table 1-10 shows other default data keywords in the file.

TABLE 1-9.   Default data keywords in flags section

Keyword	Data Item	Format	Value
:FL:	Flag list	m	*text*
:Y:	Module type	s	*text*
:MF:	MR validation	s	*yes*˜ or ˜ *no*
:MP:	MR validation program name	s	*text*
:KF:	Warning flag—keyword error	s	*yes*˜ or ˜ *no*
:KV::	Keyword validation string	s	text
:BF:	Branch flag	s	*yes*˜ or ˜ *no*
:J:	Flag for joint edit	s	*yes*˜ or ˜ *no*
:LK:	Releases locked	s	:R:...
:Q:	User-defined keyword	s	*text*
:M:	Module name	s	*text*
:FB:	Floor boundary	s	:R:
:CB:	Ceiling boundary	s	:R:
:Ds:	SID (default)	s	:I:
:ND:	Null delta flag	s	*yes*˜ or ˜ *no*

Options and Arguments

The `prs` arguments consisting of options and filenames may appear in any order, and each option applies independently to each specified file.

`-a` prints information about removed deltas, delta type = R, and about remaining deltas, delta type = D. The default is to supply information only for remaining deltas.

`-d[`*dataspec*`]` specifies the output format. The *dataspec* argument is a string of SCCS data keywords (see the "Data Keywords" section above), possibly interspersed with user-supplied text. Any data keyword may be repeated in *dataspec* as often as required.

TABLE 1-10.   Other default data keywords

Keyword	Data Item	Format	Value
:W:	`what` (CP) string	s	:Z::M:\t:I:
:A:	`what` (CP) string	s	See note 1 below.
:Z:	`what` (CP) string delimiter	s	@(#)
:F:	SCCS filename	s	*text*
:PN:	SCCS file pathname	s	*text*

Note 1: :Z::Y:˜M:˜ ::Z:

−e causes output of deltas created earlier than (and including) the delta specified by the −r parameter. Also, see the −l parameter. If both of these parameters are used, data keywords are substituted for all deltas of the SCCS file.

−l has an effect opposite to that of the −e parameter, causing output of deltas created later than the delta specified by the −r parameter.

−r*SID* prints the delta that has the ID version *SID*. The default is the most recently created delta.

filenames are .s-files (SCCS files) to be printed. If a directory is named by *filenames*, then prs acts as if all files in the directory are to be printed, except that prs silently ignores unreadable files and non-SCCS files (files lacking an .s prefix). If a hyphen (−) is used in place of *filenames*, each line of the standard input is treated as the name of an SCCS file or directory whose contents are to be printed, except that, again, prs ignores any non-SCCS or unreadable files.

Files

/tmp/pr?????

See Also

admin (CP), cdc (CP), comb (CP), delta (CP), get (CP), help (CP), rmdel (CP), sact (CP), sccsdiff (CP), unget (CP), val (CP), vc (CP), what (CP), sccsfile (SCO 1988j)

ranlib (CP)	**LIBRARY MANAGEMENT**	ranlib (CP)

Name

ranlib—convert archives to random libraries

Synopsis

ranlib *archfile* . . .

Description

The XENIX random library generator, ranlib, converts archive libraries to random libraries so that they may be loaded more rapidly. It adds a table of contents named __.SYMDEF to the beginning of the archive. Since ranlib uses ar (CP) to reconstruct the archive, the file system containing the current directory must have enough temporary file space to support the reconstruction.

The loader, ld (CP), warns if the creation date of a library dictionary is later than the modification date of the library, making it possible for a warning to be issued even if the library is only being copied.

The loader will fail if it is called without the library's first being processed or reprocessed by ranlib.

The library is first created by ar (CP) and then randomized by ranlib, making it possible for phase errors to occur.

Options and Arguments

archfile specifies the archive library to be converted into a random library.

See Also

ld (CP), ar (CP), settime (SCO 1988h)

ratfor (CP)   CONVERT RATFOR TO FORTRAN   ratfor (CP)

Name

ratfor—converts Rational FORTRAN to standard FORTRAN

Synopsis

ratfor [*option* . . .][*filename* . . .]

Description

ratfor converts Rational FORTRAN (RATFOR) to ordinary FORTRAN by substituting the control flow constructs of ordinary FORTRAN for those of RATFOR and by removing some RATFOR syntax whose purpose is to make RATFOR programs more legible. (RATFOR has control flow constructs that are essentially the same as those of the C language.)

RATFOR Control Constructs

Statement Grouping
   { *statement*; *statement*; *statement* }

Decision-Making
   if (*condition*) *statement* [else *statement*]
   switch (*integer-value*) {

```
      case integer: statement
      . . .
      [ default ] statement }
```

Loops
```
  while (condition) statement
  for (expression; condition; expression) statement
  do limits statement
  repeat statement [ until (condition) ]
  break [n]
  next [n]
```

RATFOR Syntax for Legibility

Comments
```
  # this is a comment.
```

Define
```
  define name replacement
```

Free-form Input
        multiple statements line; automatic continuation

Include
```
            include filename
```

Relationals
    $>$, $>=$, $<=$, etc. become `.GT.`, `.GE.`, and `.LE.`, etc.

Values Returned
    `return(expression)` returns an expression to the caller from a function.

Options and Arguments

    `-C` causes comments to be neatly formatted and copied to the output. Continuation lines ordinarily are indicated by an ampersand (&) in column 1.

−h converts quoted strings to 27H constructs.

−6x makes x the continuation character and puts it in column 6.

regcmp (CP) **C COMPILATION** **regcmp (CP)**

Name

regcmp—compile a regular expression

Synopsis

regcmp [−] *files*

Description

regcmp compiles regular expressions in one or more *files* and places the output in *file.i*. The resulting output is C source code. Compiled regular expressions become extern char vectors, and *file.c* files can be compiled and loaded. C programs using such regcmp output can use regex(*xyz*, *line*) to apply the regular expression *xyz* to *line*. Also, *file.i* files may be #included in C programs.

Entries in input *files* consist of a name (C variable) followed by at least one blank followed by a regular expression that is enclosed in quotes.

The regcmp command behaves like regcmp (Peterson 1991), so that it usually is not necessary to call regcmp from within a C program. This saves memory and execution time.

Options and Arguments

− places output in *file.c* instead of in *file.i*.

files contain regular expressions. Output filenames are formed by adding the extension .i or .c to the base filename.

See Also

regcmp (Peterson 1992)

rmdel (CP) **SOURCE CODE CONTROL SYSTEM** **rmdel (CP)**

Name

rmdel—remove a delta (change) from an SCCS file

Synopsis

```
rmdel -rSID filenames
```

Description

rmdel removes a specified delta from one or more SCCS files. After a specified delta is removed, its type indicator in the delta table of the specified SCCS file is changed from delta (D) to removed (R).

The delta to be removed must be a leaf delta: the most recently created delta on its branch or on the trunk of the SCCS file tree of each named SCCS file.

Removal of a delta requires the effective user to have write permission in the directory that contains the SCCS file. Furthermore, the real user must be the owner of the SCCS file and its directory or must be the creator of the delta being deleted.

The login name or the group ID of the user must be in the file's user list, or the user list must be empty.

The specified release cannot be locked. See the −1 flag of the admin command.

Options and Arguments

−rSID specifies the SCCS Identification (SID) level of the delta to be removed. The release number of the SID must be greater than or equal to the floor and less than or equal to the ceiling. Also, SID cannot specify a delta for a version being edited to create a delta. In other words, the delta cannot be specified in any existing p-file. Use of −r with rmdel is mandatory.

filenames specifies SCCS files which are to have deltas removed. If filenames specifies a directory, each file in the directory is processed by rmdel, except that rmdel silently ignores unreadable files and non-SCCS files (files lacking an s. prefix in the last part of the pathname). If − is the file specifier, rmdel treats each line of the standard input as the name of an SCCS file to process. Again, unreadable and non-SCCS files are ignored.

Files

See the "Files" subsection of the entry for the get (CP) command for a description of all SCCS files.

x-file is created during delta execution; it is renamed as an SCCS file after delta execution. See delta (CP).

z-file is created during delta execution; it is deleted after delta execution.

See Also

admin (CP), cdc (CP), comb (CP), delta (CP), get (CP), help (CP), prs (CP), sact (CP), sccsdiff (CP), unget (CP), val (CP), vc (CP), what (CP), sccsfile (SCO 1988j)

---

sact (CP)   SOURCE CODE CONTROL SYSTEM   sact (CP)

Name

sact—announce any impending deltas to an SCCS file

Synopsis

sact *filenames*

Description

sact reports about SCCS files that are being edited, i.e., it announces any impending delta. If get −e is executed without delta's subsequently being executed, a delta is impending.

The sact output for each file displays five fields separated by spaces:

Field 1 specifies the SCCS Identification String (*SID*) of an already existing delta which will be changed to produce a new delta.

Field 2 specifies the *SID* of the impending delta.

Field 3 contains the logname of the user who is creating the impending delta, i.e., who executed get −e.

Field 4 tells what date get −e was executed.

Field 5 tells what time get −e was executed.

Options and Arguments

filenames is a list of file or directory names. If *filenames* specifies a directory, each file in the directory is processed by sact, except that sact ignores unreadable files and non-SCCS files (files lacking an s. prefix in the last part of the pathname). If − is the file specifier, each line of the standard input is treated as the name of an SCCS file for sact to process. Again, sact ignores unreadable and non-SCCS files.

Files

See the "Files" subsection of the entry for the *get* (CP) command for a description of all SCCS files.

See Also

admin (CP), cdc (CP), comb (CP), delta (CP), get (CP), help (CP), prs (CP), rmdel (CP), sccsdiff (CP), unget (CP), val (CP), vc (CP), what (CP)

sccsdiff (CP) SOURCE CODE CONTROL SYSTEM sccsdiff (CP)

Name

sccsdiff—compare versions of an SCCS file

Synopsis

sccsdiff −r*SID1* −r*SID2* [-p] [-s*n*] *filenames*

Description

sccsdiff compares two versions of an SCCS file and prints (on standard output) any differences found. If no differences are found, sccsdiff prints "*filename:* No differences."

Options and Arguments

The options below apply to each specified file. All must appear before any *filenames*. Options other than −r are passed to pr (CP), which prints any differences found.

−p pipes output for each file through the XENIX pr command.

−r*SID1* and −r*SID2* specify the deltas of an SCCS file that are to be compared by sccsdiff. The two delta versions are passed to bdiff (SCO 1988j) in the order specified. These options must be the first two on the command line.

−s*n* specifies the file segment size, *n*, that bdiff (SCO 1988j) passes to diff (SCO 1988j). This option is useful if diff fails because of a too large system load.

filenames may be any SCCS files, and any number may be specified. No directory names may be used, nor may a hyphen (−) specify that lines from standard input should be treated as file or directory names.

Files

See the "Files" subsection of the entry for the *get* (CP) command for a description of all SCCS files.

/tmp/get????? contains temporary files.

See Also

admin (CP), cdc (CP), comb (CP), delta (CP), get (CP), help (CP), prs (CP), rmdel (CP), sact (CP), sccsdiff (CP), unget (CP), val (CP), vc (CP), what (CP), bdiff (SCO 1988j), pr (SCO 1988j)

sdb (CP)	DEBUGGING	sdb (CP)

Name

sdb—call a symbolic debugger

Synopsis

sdb [-w] [-W] [*objfile* [*corefile* [*dir-list*]]]

Description

sdb is a symbolic debugger that provides a controlled environment for executing C source programs and examining their core files and object files. The options used with the sdb command are described near the end of this entry.

sdb does not use the ordinary symbol table information that the a.out file contains. Instead, sdb examines special information that the compiler, cc (CP), previously produced when it was invoked with the -g or -Zi options. Use *adb* (CP) to debug any *objfile* that was created without using the -g or -Zi option of cc (CP).

When sdb is executed, it displays a prompt, after which any of the symbolic debugger commands described below may be used.

Variables and Procedures

Data stored in text sections cannot be distinguished from functions.

The sdb command writes variable names as they are written in C programs. It does not truncate names. Variables that are local to a procedure may be accessed by using the following form: *procedure*: *variable*.

Values of external variables for which no debugging information exists are assumed to be of type int. When they are printed, a warning appears before such variables.

All variables are initialized before execution of a procedure begins if the program that calls the procedure is not stopped at a breakpoint when the procedure is called. This happens, for example, when a core image is being debugged. Thus a procedure which formats core image data cannot work.

If no procedure name is given, the default procedure is the one that contains the current line. If no procedure or file is given, the default file is the current file. There is always a current file, initially set to `main( )`. The file pointed to may be changed with the source file examination commands below.

Line Numbers

There is always a current line number, initially set to the first line of `main( )`. The current line number may be changed with commands for examining source files.

Line numbers in a source program are referred to as either *file-name:number* or *procedure:number*. Whichever it is, the line number is relative to the beginning of the file. If no number is specified, the first line of the specified procedure or file is the line number used.

Line number information in functions that have been optimized cannot be relied upon. Also, information may be missing after optimization.

Arrays

The elements of a multidimensional array may be referred to by either of two forms: *variable[number1][number2]. . .* or *variable[number1, number2, . . .]*. The form *number1;number2* indicates a range of values. An asterisk used in the form *variable[*]* indicates all the values that a subscript is permitted to have. Subscripts may be omitted if they are the last of multiple subscripts specified. If trailing subscripts are omitted, all values of an array or specified subsection of an array are displayed. If all subscripts are omitted, only the address of an array or specified subsection of an array is displayed.

Structures

The `sdb` command ordinarily interprets a structure name as a set of variables. Accordingly, `sdb` displays all the elements of a structure when it is required to display a structure, except when displaying structure addresses. In this case, `sdb` displays the address of the structure.

The form *pointer[0]* is used for dereferencing pointers. Pointers to structure members are of the form *variable->member*. Structure members may be referred to by using the form *variable.member*. Combinations of the preceding forms may be used. A number may be substituted for a structure variable name. If substituted, the number is interpreted as the address of the structure and the structure template is that of the last structure referred to by `sdb`.

Stacks

A given instance of a variable on the stack may be referred to using the following form: *procedure:variable, number*. Any naming variation described in the "Variables and Procedures" section above may be used in referring to stack variables. In the above form, *number* refers to the *n*th occurrence of a specified procedure in the stack, counting down from the top, or most current, procedure. If no procedure is given, the currently executing file or procedure is used.

Addresses

Addresses may be used to specify variables. Any integer constant valid in the C language may be used as an address. Thus, addresses may be input in decimal, hexadecimal, or octal.

When a process is executing under **sdb**, every address refers to the address of the executing process. Otherwise, every address refers to either *corefile* or *objfile* (see the description of these two files in the "Options and Arguments" section below).

All appropriate values of addresses are signed 32-bit numbers so that **sdb** may be used on large files.

An address mapping for each file determines the address in that file that is associated with a written address. Two vectors represent each mapping: (*b1*, *e1*, *f1*) and (*b2*, *e2*, *f2*). The initial values of the vectors, (*b1*, *e1*, *f1*) and (*b2*, *e2*, *f2*), are suitable for a.out files and core files. If one of the files is not the expected kind, *e1* is set to the maximum file size, while *b1* and *f1* are each set to 0, allowing the whole file to be examined without address translation.

The *file-address* that corresponds to a written address is determined as follows: If *b1* is less than or equal to *address* and *address* is less than *e1*, then *file-address* equals *address*+*f1*-*b1*. Otherwise, if *b2* is less than or equal to *address* and *address* is less than *e2*, then *file-address* is equal to *address*+*f2*-*b2*. If neither of these two relations is true, the requested *address* is not allowed.

The two specified segments, (*b1*, *e1*, *f1*) and (*b2*, *e2*, *f2*), may overlap in a few cases, as with programs having separated D and I space.

Symbolic Debugger Commands

sdb commands in this section appear in boldface type. Items in brackets are optional.

The *sh* (SCO 1988j) metacharacters * and ? provide pattern matching when used within procedure or variable names in the following commands. If a procedure name is provided, only variables local to the procedure are matched. If a procedure name is not provided, global variables and variables local to the current procedure are matched. The form :*pattern* finds matching global variables only.

Controlling Source Program Execution

B prints a list of breakpoints that are currently active.

[*count*] I single-steps through *count* machine-language instructions but steps through call instructions. [*count*] i single-steps through *count* machine-language instructions. One machine-language instruction is executed if *count* is omitted.

[*count*] R runs the source program, using no arguments. If *count* is specified, it tells how many breakpoints are to be ignored.

[*count*] r *args* runs the source program, using the specified arguments. If none is specified, previously used arguments to the program are reused. An argument preceded by < or > redirects output to the standard output. If *count* is specified, it tells how many breakpoints are to be ignored.

[*count*] S single-steps through *count* lines, stepping through procedure calls. If no *count* is specified, the program executes for one line. sdb executes one line if *count* is not specified.

[*count*] s single-steps through *count* lines but does not step through procedure calls. sdb executes one line if *count* is not specified.

D deletes every breakpoint.

k kills the program being debugged.

1 prints the last line executed and makes it the current line.

[*level*] v turns off the verbose mode used in singlestepping with commands m, S, or s. If verbose mode is specified, *level* determines how verbose the reporting is. If *level* is omitted, the name of the current source file and/or the subroutine name is reported if either one changes. Each C source line is printed before it is executed if *level* is 1. Each assembler statement also is printed if *level* is 2.

[*linenumber*] a stands for "announce." The command, in effect, executes *linenumber* b 1 if *linenumber* is *proc:number* or *number*. If *number* is omitted from *proc:number*, the command, in effect, executes *proc*: b T.

[*linenumber*] b [*commands*] sets a breakpoint at *linenumber*. If *commands* is omitted, execution stops before the breakpoint and control is handed back to sdb. Otherwise, *commands* are executed when the breakpoint is found and execution resumes. Control returns to sdb instead of continuing execution if k is executed as the *command*. If a procedure name is given but no *linenumber* (for example, *proc:*), a breakpoint is placed at the first line of the procedure, even if it was compiled without using the −g option. If *linenumber* and any procedure name are omitted, sdb places a breakpoint at the current line. Multiple commands may be specified by separating them with semicolons.

[*linenumber*] c [*count*] continues program execution after a breakpoint or interrupt. Upon continuing, c ignores the signal that caused program execution to cease. If *count* is given, it tells how many breakpoints are to be ignored. If *linenumber* is given, a temporary breakpoint is inserted at that line number. The breakpoint is removed when sdb finishes.

[*linenumber*] C [*count*] continues program execution after a breakpoint or interrupt. The signal which caused program execution to cease is not reactivated. C continues, with the breakpoint that caused execution to cease reactivated. The breakpoint is removed when sdb finishes.

[*linenumber*] d removes the breakpoint at *linenumber*. If *linenumber* is omitted, breakpoints are removed interactively. The location of each breakpoint is displayed, and a line is read from standard input. If a line from standard input starts with d or y, the breakpoint is removed.

[*linenumber*] g [*count*] continues program execution after a breakpoint, resuming execution at the specified *linenumber*. The number of breakpoints to be ignored is specified by *count*.

procedure(*arg1*, *arg2*, . . .) executes *procedure*, using the specified arguments, and prints the value returned by the procedure according to the default format, d. Executing this command requires the program to have been previously compiled using the −g option. The *procedure* arguments may be characters, integers, or string constants, or names of variables accessible from the current procedure.

procedure(*arg1*, *arg2*, . . .)/m executes *procedure*, using the specified arguments, and prints the value returned by the *procedure* according to the format specified by m. The default format is d. Executing this command requires the program to have previously been compiled using the −g option. The *procedure* arguments may be characters, integers, or string constants, or names of variables accessible from the current procedure.

variable$m [*count*] single-steps through instructions until *variable* gets a new value. The *variable* must be accessible from within the current procedure. *count* specifies the how many instructions to single-step through; *count* is infinite if *count* is omitted.

Debugger-Debugging Commands
The following two commands are for use in debugging the debugger.
Q prints a list of files and procedures being debugged.
V prints the version number of sdb.

Examining Data in Programs
Most commands for examining data in the program may have length specifiers, *l*, and format specifiers, *m*.
A given length specifier may result in truncation of output variables. The possible values of *l* are as follows:

b 1 byte
h 2 bytes (half a word)
l 4 bytes (a long word)

Any length specifier can be used effectively with the c, d, u, o, and x format specifiers below. The possible format specifiers, *m*, are as follows:

c character
d decimal
u decimal, unsigned
o octal
x hexadecimal
f 32-bit floating point, single precision
g 64-bit floating point, double precision
s prints characters starting at the address pointed to by *variable*; assume that *variable* is a string pointer.
i disassembles machine-language instructions and prints addresses both numerically and symbolically.

linenumber?*lm* prints (under the control of the format specification *lm*) the value at the address from a.out or i space specified by *linenumber* under the control of format *lm*. The default format is i.

linenumber=*lm* prints (under the control of the format specification *lm*) the address of *linenumber*. The default format specification is lx (4 bytes, hex).

number=*lm* prints (under the control of the format specification *lm*) the value of *number*. The default format specification is lx (4 bytes, hex). This command converts data between decimal, hexadecimal, and octal.

T prints the top line of the stack trace.

t prints a stack trace.

variable!*value* assigns a *value* (number, or character constant, or variable) to *variable*. C language conventions govern any type conversions necessary to make the assignment. Numbers are treated as integers if no exponent or decimal point is used. Otherwise, they are treated as type double variables. Registers are treated as integers. Character constants are designated by '*character*. Expressions producing more than one *value*, for example, structures or unions, are not permitted. On the other hand, *variable* may be an expression indicating more than one value, for example, a structure or array. The address of *variable* or any variable is treated as having type int.

variable/*clm* displays memory locations. The display is controlled by values of *variable*, c, l, and m. The numeric count, c, determines the number of units of memory to display. The length, l, specifies the length of units of memory to be output, starting at the address implied by *variable* and using the output format *m*. If *l* or *m* is omitted, s db selects a format suitable for the *variable* type declared in the program. If *m* is specified, but not *leng*, the default length of *variable* is 2 bytes. If a numeric length specifier is used for *m*, s db prints that many characters. Otherwise, s db prints successive characters until it encounters a null byte or until it prints 128 characters.

variable = *lm* prints (under the control of the format specification *lm*) the address of *variable*, providing a convenient way to convert between decimal, hexadecimal, and octal. The default format specification is *lx* (4 bytes, hex).

X prints current machine-language instruction.

x prints machine registers and the current machine-language instruction.

Examining Source Files

The debugger maintains the variables *current-line* and *current-file*. If *corefile* (see *corefile* in the "Options and Arguments" section below) exists, these two variables are initially set to the line and file that contain the source statement at which the process terminated. Otherwise, the two variables are set to indicate the first line of main(). Some of the following commands can change *current-file* and *current-line*:

/ *regular expression*[/] searches forward from the current line, looking for a line containing a string that matches *regular expression*. See ed(SCO 1988j). The trailing / may be omitted.

? *regular expression*[?] searches backward from the current line, looking for a line containing a string that matches *regular expression*. See ed (SCO 1988j). The trailing ? may be omitted.

count + advances by *count* lines to the new current line and prints the new current line. The default is one line if *count* is omitted.

count - retreats by *count* lines to the new current line and prints the new current line. The default is one line if *count* is omitted.

e displays the name of the current procedure and file.

e *filename* sets the current file to *filename* and makes the current line number be the first line in *filename*.

e *procedure* makes the current source file be the file that contains *procedure*. The first line of the new file becomes the current line.

number sets the current line number to *number* and prints the new line.

p prints the current line.

w prints a window consisting of the 10 lines surrounding the current line.

z prints the current line and the following nine lines. The last line printed becomes the new current line.

Miscellaneous Commands

! *command* causes *command* to be passed to sh(SCO 1988j), the shell, where it is interpreted.

end-of-file scrolls and prints the next 10 lines of data, instructions, or source, depending on what was printed last. The end-of-file character usually is Ctrl-D.

< *file* reads commands from *file* until it encounters an end-of-file character, after which it continues to read commands from standard input. This command may not be nested. Thus < may not appear in the file as a command. If a command given in *file* or standard input directs sdb to display a variable, the variable name is also displayed.

newline advances the current line by one and prints the new current line if the previous line displayed a source line. Otherwise, if a memory location was printed by the previous command, the next memory location is printed.

q exits sdb.

' ' *string* prints *string*. The command recognizes C escape sequences in *string* like \ *character*, where *character* is nonnumeric.

Options and Arguments

corefile is a core image file generated after *objfile* is executed. The core file does not need to be present. The default core image file is core. If – is specified in place of *corefile*, it causes sdb to ignore any core image file.

dir-list is a colon-separated list of directories containing the source files used in building *objfile*.

objfile is an executable program file which has usually been compiled using the −Zi or −g (debug) option of the compiler. If −Zi or −g was not used, sdb can still examine *objfile* and debug it, though debugging capabilities will be limited. The default *objfile* is a.out.

Files

```
a.out
core
```

See Also

cc (CP), sh (SCO 1988j), a.out (SCO 1988j), core (SCO 1988j)

size (CP)	OBJECT FILE MANIPULATION	size (CP)

Name

size—print the section size of common object files

Synopsis

size [-n] [-f] [-o] [-x] [-V] *filenames*

Description

The size command prints the number of bytes in each loaded section of the specified common object file(s). The command reports the size of the text section (executable code), the data section (initialized data), and the bss section (uninitialized data). It also prints their sum in both decimal and hexadecimal. However, since the size of the bss section is unknown until link time, size does not report the true size of objects before linking takes place.

Archive files may be input to size. This creates a size report for all archive members.

Options and Arguments

filenames is a.out unless some other filename is specified.

See Also

as (CP), cc (CP), ld (CP), a.out (SCO 1988j), ar (SCO 1988j)

---

spline (CP)   MATHEMATICAL UTILITY   spline (CP)

Name

spline—interpolate a smooth curve

Synopsis

spline [*option* . . .]

Description

spline accepts pairs of numbers from the standard input as the abscissas and ordinates of a function. From this input it creates a similar set of points, approximately equally spaced and including the input set, and sends the similar set of points to the standard output. The output is a cubic spline with two continuous derivatives. It has enough points to appear smooth when plotted. If the data are not strictly monotone in x, spline merely reproduces the input without interpolating any points.

spline can accept up to 1000 input points.

Options and Arguments

$-a$ automatically supplies abscissas, with spacing either being given by the next argument or assumed to be 1 if the next argument is not a number.

$-k$ causes a constant k, used in the boundary value computation

$$y_0'' = ky_1', \ldots y_n'' = ky_{n-1}'$$

to be set by the next argument. The default value of k is 0.

$-n$ causes output points to be spaced so that there are approximately n intervals between the upper and lower limits of x. The default is $n = 100$.

$-p$ causes the derivatives at the ends to be matched (output is periodic). Ordinarily, the first and last values should agree.

$-x$ causes the next one (or two) arguments to be used as the lower (and upper) limits of x. Automatic abscissas begin at the lower limit (default is 0).

strings (CP)   OBJECT FILE MANIPULATION   strings (CP)

Name

strings—look for ASCII strings in an object file

Synopsis

strings [-] [-o] [-number] filename . . .

Description

strings searches binary file(s) for ASCII strings consisting of sequences of four or more printing characters ending with a newline or null character. strings is useful for locating random object files.

Options and Arguments

- causes strings to search other sections of object files in addition to the data section.

-number specifies the minimum length of strings to be searched for (default is 4).

-o displays the decimal offset of each string found in filename, followed by the string itself.

filename is the input object file.

See Also

hd (SCO 1988j), od (SCO 1988j)

| strip (CP) | OBJECT FILE MANIPULATION | strip (CP) |

Name

strip—strip the symbol table and line numbers from file(s)

Synopsis

strip [-MNSdehrstx] *filename* . . .

Description

strip deletes the symbol table and line number information (relocation bits) from the specified common object files, including archive files. This reduces the file storage overhead used by an object file. The −s option of ld has the same effect as strip.

Once a file is stripped, the sdb command can no longer be used on the file. Thus strip is useful for preparing production modules after debugging and testing are finished.

If strip processes an archive file, it will remove all the local symbols from any a.out format files in the archive. Before the archive can be link-edited by ld (CP), the archive symbol table must be restored, using the ar (CP) command with an −s option; strip indicates if this restoration is required.

Libraries such as those in /lib have no need for local symbols. The size of such archives can be reduced and link editing can be speeded up if local symbols are removed.

Options and Arguments

The following options control the amount of information stripped from the symbol table:

−M strips every memory image segment.

−N strips every nonmemory image segment.

−S strips only the segment table.

−h strips the header and the extended header.

−r strips all relocation except the short form of x.out.

−s strips the symbol table.

−x strips all relocation information.

filename is the common object file from which symbol table information is to be stripped.

Files

/tmp/stm* is a temporary file.

See Also

ar (CP), as (CP), cc (CP), ld (CP), a.out (SCO 1988j), ar (SCO 1988j), tmpnam (Peterson 1992)

tic (CP)   TERMINAL INFORMATION   tic (CP)

Name

tic—compile *terminfo* file

Synopsis

tic [-v[*n*]] [-p *permlist*] *filename*

Description

tic compiles terminal descriptions contained in the terminfo (SCO 1988j) data base. It places its results in the directory /usr/lib/terminfo, where they are available as input to the routines in curses (Peterson 1992).

The tic command gets binary data from /usr/lib/terminfo to complete an entry that it is busy compiling when it finds a use = *entry* field in the entry. The command uses entries created from *filename* first, and it duplicates the capabilities in *entry* except those explicitly defined in the current entry. After searching the current file, tic searches the master file, ./terminfo.src.

If the environment variable TERMINFO is set, tic puts its results there rather than in /usr/lib/terminfo.

Some numeric limits on tic are as follows: There may be no more than 4096 bytes in total compiled entries. The *filename* field (see below) must be 128 bytes or less.

Options and Arguments

-p *permlist* causes tic to create *permlist*, a permissions file for use with fixperm (SCO 1988h). Avoid using the -p option because its functionality may change in future XENIX releases.

-v*n* causes verbose output trace information (to standard error) showing tic's progress. Ten different levels of detail are possible, each specified by an integer value of *n* between 1 and 10, with *n* = 10 giving the most detail. The default is 1.

filename contains terminfo (Peterson 1992) descriptions in source format, each description describing the capabilities of one particular terminal.

Files

/usr/lib/terminfo/*/* contains the compiled terminal data base describing terminal capabilities.

See Also

curses (Peterson 1992), fixperm (SCO 1988h), terminfo (Peterson 1992), terminfo (SCO 1988j)

---

time (CP)   **PROFILING**   **time (CP)**

Name

time—times execution of a command

Synopsis

time *command*

Description

time prints the amount of time spent executing a specified command, the elapsed time during a command, and the amount of time spent in the system. The times are printed on the stderr.

Options and Arguments

command specifies the command to be executed

See Also

time (Peterson 1992)

Name

tsort—topological sort

Synopsis

tsort [*filename*]

Description

tsort generates (on standard output) a totally ordered list. The total ordering of items is consistent with a partial ordering of items in the input file.

The input is pairs of nonempty strings separated by blanks. Pairs of differing items indicate the ordering. Pairs of identical items merely indicate presence, not ordering.

tsort uses a quadratic algorithm and thus is slow if the input list is large.

Diagnostic Messages

"Odd data: there is an odd number of fields in the input file" is self-explanatory.

Options and Arguments

filename contains the input to tsort. If no *filename* is specified, input comes from the standard input.

See Also

lorder (CP)

unget (CP)   SOURCE CODE CONTROL SYSTEM   unget (CP)

Name

unget—undo a prior get of an SCCS file

Synopsis

unget [-r*SID*] [-s] [-n] *filenames*

Description

unget reverses the effect of a get −c executed on one or more files before the intended new delta was created.

Options and Arguments

The following options affect each named file independently:

−n retains file(s) retrieved by get (CP). The default is that the file is removed from the current directory.

−rSID specifies which delta [the SID specified by a previous get (CP) as the new delta] is no longer intended. The r option need not be specified if only one get by a user (login name) is outstanding on an SCCS file. The unget command will complain if a needed SID is omitted from the command line or if an ambiguous SID is given.

−s suppresses display (on standard output) of the SID of the new delta about to be created.

filenames specifies the SCCS file(s) which unget is to process. If filenames specifies a directory, unget processes each file in the directory except that unget ignores non-SCCS and unreadable files. If filenames is −, unget treats each line of standard input as the name of an SCCS file to process.

Files

See the "Files" subsection of the entry for the get (CP) command for a description of all SCCS files.

See Also

admin (CP), cdc (CP), comb (CP), delta (CP), get (CP), help (CP), prs (CP), rmdel (CP), sact (CP), sccsdiff (CP), val (CP), vc (CP), what (CP)

---

val (CP)   **SOURCE CODE CONTROL SYSTEM**   **val (CP)**

Name

val—validate an SCCS file

Synopsis

val −

or

val [−s] [−rSID] [−mname] [−ytype] filenames

Description

val determines if certain characteristics of designated SCCS file(s) match those specified by the options of the **val** command.

val returns an 8-bit error code upon exit. Since multiple files may be specified on a **val** command line, and since **val** can process multiple command lines, **val** returns a logical OR of the code created for each file and command line it processes. A return code of zero means that every file matched the specified characteristics.

Each bit set in an individual 8-bit error code indicates a specific error. Set bits are interpreted as follows, moving from left to right:

Bit 0 set means that a file argument is missing.
Bit 1 set means that an option is unknown or duplicated.
Bit 2 set means that an SCCS file is corrupted.
Bit 3 set means that a file is not SCCS or cannot be opened.
Bit 4 set means that an *SID* is invalid or ambiguous.
Bit 5 set means that an *SID* is nonexistent.
Bit 6 set means that a %Y%, −y mismatch occurred.
Bit 7 set means that a %M%, −m mismatch occurred.

Options and Arguments

The effects of the following options apply independently to each file specified. The options may appear in any order.

− causes **val** to read the standard input until it encounters an end-of-file condition (CTRL-D). **val** processes each line of standard input independently as if it were a separate command list. This allows one **val** to have different values for options and filenames. The − option is treated differently by **val** than by other SCCS commands. Also, it is not used together with other options of **val**.

−m*name* compares the value of *name* with the SCCS %M% keyword in *filenames*, i.e, the value of *name* is compared with the value set by the −m flag of **admin** (CP).

−r*SID* specifies the delta whose existence **val** is to check for. The command determines whether the *SID* is ambiguous or invalid before checking whether the *SID* actually exists. An *SID* may be ambiguous because it does not physically exist but implies *SID*'s which may exist; for example, r1 does not exist, but it implies r1.1, r1.2, and r1.3, which do exist. Also, an *SID* may be ambiguous because it cannot exist as a valid *SID*; for example, r2.0 and r2.1.0 are invalid. **val** checks whether a valid, unambiguous *SID* actually exists.

−s suppresses diagnostic messages. Otherwise, such messages are sent to the standard output file for any error found while processing each file listed on each command line.

−y*type* compares the value of *type* with the SCCS %Y% keyword in *filenames*, i.e, the value of *type* is compared with the value set by the −t flag of admin (CP).

filenames specifies SCCS files to be processed by val. Up to 50 files can be specified on a val command line. Anything more causes a core dump.

Files

See the "Files" subsection of the entry for the get (CP) command for a description of all SCCS files.

See Also

admin (CP), cdc (CP), comb (CP), delta (CP), get (CP), help (CP), prs (CP), rmdel (CP), sact (CP), sccsdiff (CP), unget (CP), vc (CP), what (CP)

what (CP)   SOURCE CODE CONTROL SYSTEM   what (CP)

Name

what—identify the SCCS file by searching for a pattern

Synopsis

what [−s] *filenames*

Description

what searches specified files for any occurrences of the pattern ((@(#)) substituted for %Z% by get (CP). It prints out text following the pattern until it encounters the first ~, null character, >, newline, or \. As an example, if the C program in file.c contains the line

char commnt[ ] = "@(#)comments";

and file.c is compiled, yielding file.o and a.out, then if

what file.c file.o a.out

is executed, the what command will print

```
file.c  comments
file.o  comments
a.out   comments
```

what is used in searching for the identifyimg information that get automatically inserts in files.

Diagnostic Messages
The command returns 1 if no matches were found. Otherwise, it returns 0.

Options and Arguments

filenames specifies the files to be searched.

Files

See the "Files" subsection of the entry for the get (CP) command for a description of all SCCS files.

See Also

admin (CP), cdc (CP), comb (CP), delta (CP), get (CP), help (CP), prs (CP), rmdel (CP), sact (CP), sccsdiff (CP), unget (CP), vc (CP), what (CP)

---

xref (CP)   **DEBUGGING AIDS**   **xref (CP)**

Name

xref—cross-reference C programs

Synopsis

xref [filename ...]

Description

xref reads the specified files and prints a cross-reference listing consisting of lines having the following form:

identifier *filename* line-numbers

xref marks function definitions with a plus sign (+) preceding the line number.

Options and Arguments

filename specifies the files for which a cross-reference listing will be printed. The default file is standard input.

See Also

cref (CP)

---

xstr (CP)	C STRING MANIPULATION	xstr (CP)

Name

xstr—extracts strings from C programs

Synopsis

xstr [-c] [-] [*filename*]

Description

xstr hashes strings from a program into a file. The strings are replaced by references to this common area. This implements shared constant strings. It is best if they are read-only. If, after the C preprocessor is run, macro definitions yield strings or conditional code contains strings that may not be needed, run xstr.

A command sequence for executing xstr after the C preprocessor is invoked is

```
cc -E filename.c | xstr -c -
cc -c x.c
mv x.o filname.o
```

Since xstr does not touch the *strings* file unless a new item is added, make (Peterson 1991) does not need to remake xs.o unless it has been otherwise altered.

A command having the form

xstr -c *filename1*, *filename2*, *filename3* ...

creates an xs.c file that declares the common xstr space of several files from a large program after all components have been compiled. The resulting xs.c file should be compiled and loaded with the other parts of the program. Space and swap overhead can be saved if the array is made read-only.

A command having the form

xstr -c *filename*

extracts strings from the C source in *filename* and replaces string references by expressions having the form (&xstr[*number*]). A declaration of xstr is prepended to the file. The text resulting from this extraction is put in the x.c file for compilation. Any string in this file is put in the *strings* data base unless it is already there. No changes are caused by strings which are either repeated strings or suffixes of existing strings. However, if a string is a suffix of another string in the data base and the shorter of the two strings is encountered first by xstr, both strings will be put in the data base.

A command having the form

xstr *filename*

that specifies a single file creates x.c and xs.c files, as the two commands above do, but does not affect any *strings* file in the same directory.

Options and Arguments

– causes xstr to read from standard input.

–c causes xstr to read from the specified files.

filename is the C source file from which strings are to be extracted.

Files

strings contains the data base of strings.

x.c contains modified C source code.

xs.c contains the C source for a definition of the array "xstr".

/tmp/xs* contains a temporary file when "xstr name" does not touch strings.

See Also

mkstr (CP)

Source

This utility was created at the University of California at Berkeley.

Name

yacc—yet another compiler-compiler

Synopsis

yacc [-vd] [-S[amsrnilw]*num*] *filename*

Description

The yacc command transforms a context-free grammar contained in a specification file, *filename*, into a set of tables for input to a parser which executes an LR(1) parsing operation. The parser, created by yacc, is a finite-state machine with a stack.

Each state of the parser has its own integer label. The current state of the parser is always on the top of the stack. The parser can look ahead, reading and remembering the next token in the input (the look-ahead token). The parser starts with only state 0 in the stack and with no look-ahead token having been read.

The parser can perform only four different actions: shift, reduce, accept, and error. Using one or another of these actions, the parser makes a single step from one state to another as follows:

It examines its current state and decides if a look-ahead token is required to choose an action. If a look-ahead token is needed, the parser calls yylex to get it.

The current state and the look-ahead token (if required) jointly determine the next action of the parser, possibly causing the look-ahead token to be processed or ignored, or states to be popped off the stack or pushed on.

The shift action is the action the parser most frequently takes. Invariably, a look-ahead token is available when a shift is performed. In some parser state, say 20, there may be an action, say,

IF shift 30

stating that if the look-ahead token is IF, the current state, 20, is pushed down into the stack, and state 30 is put on the top of the stack (becomes the current state). The look-ahead token is discarded.

The reduce action prevents the stack from growing large without bound.

The action goes back to an earlier state of the stack, to a point where the parser first found the right side of a given rule. The parser then acts as if it had seen the left side of the rule at that time.

The **accept** action is taken when the look-ahead token is the end marker. It indicates that the parser has succeeded in examining the entire input and the input matches the specification.

The **error** action is taken when the parser reaches a point where it cannot continue parsing according to specifications.

The grammar may be ambiguous, i.e., there may be input strings that can be structured in more than one way. Two disambiguating rules are used to remove such ambiguities:

- Do the **shift** when there is a **shift-reduce** conflict.
- Reduce by the earlier grammar rule to resolve a **reduce-reduce** conflict.

The output file, `y.tab.c`, produced by `yacc` must be compiled, yielding a `yparse` program. This, in turn, must be loaded together with three other programs: `main`; `ylex`, the lexical analyzer program; and `yerror`, an error-handling routine. These programs must be supplied by the user; `yylex` can be created by `lex` (CP).

Diagnostic Messages

If some rules cannot be reached from the start symbol, `yacc` reports this. Also, `yacc` reports (on standard output) the number of **reduce-reduce** and **shift-reduce** conflicts it finds. It puts a more detailed report in the `y.output` file.

Options and Arguments

`-d` creates `y.tab.h`, a file containing `#define` statements that associate token names declared by users with token codes assigned by `yacc`. This lets the token codes be accessed by source files other than `y.tab.c`.

`-v` creates `y.output`, a file containing a description of parsing tables and a report of conflicts caused by ambiguities in the grammar.

`-S` controls internal `yacc` values when combined with one of the keyletters in the following table. `-S` may be combined with more than one keyletter from the following table, but each such pair must be given separately, and each pair must have its own *num* value.

Flag	Action Controlled	Default
`-Sanum`	actions per rule (number of)	4000
`-Smnum`	space for optimizer	5200

-Ss*num*	states (number of)	600
-Sr*num*	rules (number of)	300
-Sn*num*	nonterminal symbols (number of)	200
-Si*num*	literals and identifiers (number of)	4000
-Sl*num*	look-ahead sets (number of)	450
-Sw*num*	working sets (number of)	250

filename is a specification file containing rules consisting of chains of definitions and alternate definitions written in Backus-Naur form. The rules are accompanied by C code to be invoked when tokens in the input match the rules. Apart from *file*, filenames (y.tab.h, y.tab.c, and y.output) are fixed, permitting only one yacc process to be executing in a directory at a time.

Files

y.output
y.tab.c
y.tab.h defines token names.
yacc.acts contains temporary files.
yacc.tmp contains temporary files.
/usr/lib/yaccpar contains parser prototype for C programs.

See Also

lex (CP)

Part II

DOS Cross Development Services

This chapter consists of three main parts:

- An explanation of the format of the entries that describe system calls used in DOS cross development,
- A system call classification section (page 118) that helps you quickly find the appropriate system call for your purpose, and
- the descriptive entries themselves.

Format of System Call Descriptions

The descriptive entries consist of up to eight separate sections: Name, Synopsis, Description, Arguments, Normal Completion: Value Returned, Error Condition: Value Returned, See Also, and Example.

Name
Each entry describing a system call begins with the name of the call, followed by a brief phrase describing its purpose.

117

Synopsis

The synopsis subsection of each entry lists header files which must be included, and it shows the system call and its arguments.

Description

Each description contains general details about the system call.

Arguments

Where possible (and it nearly always is), all of the information about each argument of a system call is put in this subsection. The descriptions of arguments are sorted in ASCII order of the argument names as these are given in the synopsis. Usually, when information about an argument must appear in other subsections or in the material about another argument, the argument description will point to such material.

Normal Completion: Value Returned

All of the values returned by DOS cross development system calls are described in this section.

Error Condition: Value Returned

Many of the system calls in this chapter have one or more possible error conditions. The presence of an error condition is indicated by a return value that is otherwise never returned. This value almost always is either − 1 or the NULL pointer. Additionally, for many of the system services, the error number is made available in the external variable `errno`. Since `errno` is not cleared by calls that succeed, the value of `errno` should not be tested unless the presence of an error condition has been indicated by an error return value.

The `#include` file `<errno.h>` defines the error number corresponding to each error condition, as well as its associated name.

See Also

This section of each system call description points to related commands.

class (DOS)   SYSTEM CALL CLASSIFICATION   class (DOS)

This section classifies system calls that are generally useful in cross development of DOS software. The page reference following each description in the list points to the entry that describes that system service.

Address Register Values

FP__OFF   returns the offset of a long pointer   136

| FP_SEG | returns the segment of a long pointer | 136 |
| segread | gets segment register values | 155 |

Directory Operations
mkdir	creates a new directory	150
rename	renames a specified file or directory	153
rmdir	deletes a specified directory	154

DOS System Calls
bdos	invokes a DOS system call	121
dosexterr	gets DOS error messages	129
intdos	invokes a DOS system call	143
intdosx	invokes a DOS system call	144

File and Stream Operations

Files
eof	tests if end-of-file has been reached	130
filelength	gets file length	134
isatty	test if *handle* is associated with character device	145
setmode	sets the translation mode of a file	156
sopen	opens a file for shared I/O	157
tell	gets the current position of a file pointer	169

Streams
| fclose | closes the specified stream | 132 |
| fcloseall | closes all streams except standard streams | 132 |

Input/Output Operations

Input
Console
cgets	gets a string from the console	122
cscanf	gets data from the console under format control	126
getch	gets a character from the console	138
getche	gets a character from the console and echoes it	139
kbhit	checks the console for a keystroke	147
Port
| inp | reads a byte from a specified port | 140 |
Stream
| fgetc | gets a character from input *stream* | 133 |
| fgetchar | gets a character from *stdin* | 133 |

Output
Buffers

`flushall`   flushes every output buffer   135

Console

`cprintf`   formats and prints characters to the console   123
`cputs`   puts a null-terminated string to the console   126
`putch`   writes a character to the console   153
`ungetch`   pushes a character back to the console buffer   171

Port

`outp`   writes a byte to a specified port   152

Stream

`fputc`   puts a character to a *stream*   137
`fputchar`   puts a character to `stdout`   137

Move Bytes in Memory
`movedata`   copies bytes from a specified location   150

Process Control
`exit`   terminates the calling process   131
`spawnl`   creates and executes a new process   160
`spawnvp`   creates and executes a new process   160

Software Interrupts
`int86`   executes an 8086 software interrupt   140
`int86x`   execute an 8086 software interrupt   141

Variables

Conversions
`itoa`   converts an integer to a character string   146
`ltoa`   converts a long integer to a character string   149
`ultoa`   converts a long integer to a character string   170

Integer Operations
`labs`   returns the absolute value of a long integer   148

String Operations
`strlen`   returns the length of a character string   165
`strlwr`   converts uppercase characters to lowercase   166
`strrev`   reverses the order of characters in a string   167

strset   sets all characters in a string to the same character   167
strupr   converts lowercase characters to uppercase   168

bdos (DOS)	DOS SYSTEM CALLS	bdos (DOS)

Name

bdos—invokes a specified DOS system call

Synopsis

```
#include <dos.h>

int bdos(dosfnc, dosdx, dosal);
int dosfnc;
unsigned int dosdx;
unsigned int dosal;
```

Description

bdos executes an INT 21H instruction to invoke a specified MS-DOS system call after loading the DX and AL registers. The purpose of bdos is to invoke system calls that have no arguments or that take arguments in the DX (DH, DL) and/or AL registers.

Compile bdos with the −dos flag.

Arguments

dosal specifies the value to be placed in the AL register.
dosdx specifies the value to be placed in the DX register.
dosfnc specifies the MS-DOS system call to be invoked by bdos.

Normal Completion: Value Returned

bdos returns the value in the AX register upon successful completion.

Error Condition: Value Returned

None. The bdos call should not be used to invoke MS-DOS calls that indicate errors by setting the carry flag. Because C programs cannot access this flag, the return value cannot be determined. Use intdos if the status of the carry flag is needed.

See Also

intdos (DOS), intdosx (DOS)

cgets (DOS)   CONSOLE INPUT   cgets (DOS)

Name

cgets—gets a string from the console.

Synopsis

```
#include <conio.h>

char *cgets(string);
char *string;
```

Description

cgets reads a string of characters from the console and stores it in the specified *string*. cgets reads characters until it reads a carriage return/linefeed combination (CR-LF), or until it reads a specified number of characters. If cgets reads a CR-LF combination, it replaces the CR-LF with a null character ($\backslash$0) before storing it.

Compile cgets with the −dos flag.

Arguments

string is a pointer to a character array whose first element, *string[0]*, contains the maximum length, in characters, of the string to be read by cgets. cgets stores the actual length of the string in *string[1]* and starts storing the string at *string[2]*. The array has to have enough elements to contain the string, a terminating null character '$\backslash$0', and two additional bytes.

Normal Completion: Value Returned

cgets returns a pointer to the beginning of the string.

Error Condition: Value Returned

No error is returned.

See Also

`getch` (DOS), `getche` (DOS)

cprintf (DOS)	**CONSOLE OUTPUT**	cprintf (DOS)

Name

`cprintf`—formats and prints characters to the console.

Synopsis

```
#include <conio.h>

int cprintf(format[arg1 . . .]);
char *format;
```

Description

`cprintf` formats and prints a set of characters and values to the console, using `putch` to output characters.

`cprintf` does not translate linefeed (LF) characters into carriage return/linefeed combinations (CR-LF) on output. Use `fprintf` (Peterson 1992), `printf` (Peterson 1992), or `sprintf` (Peterson 1991) instead if such translation is required.

Compile `cprintf` with the −dos flag.

Arguments

[*arg1* . . .] specifies argument(s) to be converted according to the format specifications in *format*.

format is a character string containing two kinds of objects: plain characters and conversion specifications. Plain characters are simply copied to the output stream. Each conversion specification causes zero or more *args* to be fetched, converted, and sent to the output stream. If all conversion specifications in the *format* are used up while any *args* remain, the remaining *args* are ignored.

Each conversion specification in *format* is preceded by %. After %, the following conversion specifications appear in the sequence shown below:

flags modify the meaning of a conversion specification. One or more of the following flags may be present:

− causes the result of a conversion to be left justified.

+ causes the result of a signed conversion always to begin with a sign (− or +).

blank prepends a blank to the result of a signed conversion if the first character is not a sign. If both the blank flag and the + flag appear, the blank flag will be ignored.

\# specifies an alternate conversion result as follows:

- Has no effect for c, d, s, or u conversions,
- Increases precision to force the first digit of the result of o conversions to be zero,
- Prepends 0x to the result of an x conversion if the result is non-zero, or
- Forces the result of e, E, f, g, and G conversions to contain a decimal point, even when no digits follow the point. For g and G conversions, no trailing zeroes will be removed.

field width is an optional decimal digit string that specifies minimum field width. Any converted value that has fewer characters than the field width will be padded to the full field width. Padding will be on the left unless the left-adjustment flag (−) described above is used. If the field width specifier is preceded by a blank (for example, % 5), the value will be padded by blanks. If the field width specifier is preceded by a zero (for example, %05), the converted value will be padded by zeroes. Numeric conversions are the only conversions that may be padded by zeroes.

The field width may be determined by an asterisk (*) instead of a digit string. If so, an integer *arg* gives the field width. Any *arg* that is actually converted is fetched after the conversion character is examined, so any *arg*s that specify field width must appear before the *arg* that is to be converted.

precision is a period (.) followed by a decimal digit string. The precision determines the following:

- The number of digits appearing after the decimal point for e and f conversions, or
- The minimum number of digits appearing in d, o, u, x, or X conversions, or
- The maximum number of digits which are to be printed from a string for s conversions, or
- The maximum number of significant digits for g conversions. A null digit string is taken to be zero, but in no case does a nonexistent or small field width force truncation of a field. If the result of a conversion is wider than the field, the field is expanded to contain the result of the conversion.

l-specifier (optional) specifies that the following d, o, u, x, or X conversion character applies to a long integer.

conversion character
    c prints the character *arg*.
    d, o, u, x, or X converts the integer *arg* to

- signed decimal (d),
- Unsigned octal (o),
- Unsigned decimal (u), or
- Hexadecimal (x or X). The letters ABCDEF are used for X conversion, while the letters abcdef are used for x conversion. The precision (see *precision* above) determines the minimum number of digits to be printed. The default if no precision is specified is 1. Any value that can be expressed by fewer digits than the precision calls for will be expanded with leading zeroes. If a zero value is converted with a precision of zero, the result is a null string unless the # flag is used (see *flags* above) and the conversion is o, x, or X.

e, E converts a double or float *arg* to the style "$[-]d.ddde+dd$" or "$[-]d.ddde-dd$". One digit appears before the decimal point, and the precision specifier determines how many digits appear after the decimal point. Six digits are output if the precision specifier is missing. No decimal point appears if the precision is specified to be zero. The exponent always has two digits, except that if the value to be printed is $1E + 100$ or more, additional exponent digits will be printed as required. If the E format specifier is used, the exponent of the converted number will be preceded by E instead of e.

f converts a double or float *arg* to decimal having the style "$[-]ddd.ddd$". The number of digits following the decimal point is determined by the precision specification. Six digits are output if the precision specifier is missing. No decimal point appears if the precision is specified to be zero.

g, G prints the float or double *arg* in style e or f (in style E if the format code is G). Style e is used only if the exponent of the conversion result is greater than the precision or less than -4. The precision specifier determines the number of significant digits. A decimal appears only if it is followed by a digit, and trailing zeroes are deleted.

s causes *arg* to be treated as a string pointer. Characters from the string are printed until the number of characters indicated by the precision specifier are printed or until a null character ($\backslash 0$) is encountered. All characters until the first null character are printed if the precision specifier is missing.

% prints a % without converting any argument.

Normal Completion: Value Returned

cprintf returns a count of the number of characters printed.

Error Condition: Value Returned

None.

See Also

fprintf (Peterson 1992), printf (Peterson 1992), sprintf (Peterson 1992)

cputs (DOS)	CONSOLE OUTPUT	cputs (DOS)

Name

cputs — puts a null-terminated string to the console

Synopsis

```
#include <conio.h>

void cputs(string);
char *string;
```

Description

cputs writes the specified null-terminated string to the console without automatically appending a carriage return/linefeed combination (CR-LF) to the string after writing.

Compile cputs with the −dos flag.

Arguments

string points to a null-terminated string that will be written to the console.

Normal Completion: Value Returned

No value is returned.

Error Condition: Value Returned

No error value is returned.

See Also

putch (DOS)

cscanf (DOS)	CONSOLE INPUT	cscanf (DOS)

Name

cscanf—gets data from console under format control

Synopsis

```
#include <conio.h>

int cscanf(format[arg1 . . .]);
char *format;
```

Description

cscanf reads data from the console to the locations specified by the arguments (if any). It uses the getche(DOS) function to read characters.
Compile cscanf with the −dos flag.

Arguments

[arg1 . . .] indicates where converted input is to be stored. Each arg points to a variable that has a type corresponding to a type specifier in format.

format is a string that consists of conversion characters that control the conversion of input. The conversion characters may be:

- Ordinary characters other than %, each of which must match the next character in the input stream, or
- Blanks, newlines, or tabs which cause input to be read until the next non-white-space character is encountered, or
- Conversion specifications consisting of the % character, followed by an optional assignment suppression character, followed by an optional specifier of maximum field width, followed by a conversion character.

A conversion character controls conversion of the next input field. The result of each conversion is put in the variable that is pointed to by the corresponding argument unless assignment is suppressed by an asterisk (*). Suppression of assignment enables description of input fields which are to be skipped. Conversion characters may be one of the following characters:

% causes a single % to be expected as the next input. No assignment is done.

c causes a character to be expected as the next input. The corresponding arg should be a character pointer. Space characters are not skipped, contrary to normal practice. If space characters are to be skipped, the %1s conversion specification should be used. If a field width is specified, the arg corresponding to the specification should be a character array. The number of characters corresponding to the field width is read.

d causes a decimal integer input to be expected as the next input. The corresponding arg should be an integer pointer. The d specifier may be capitalized. It also may be preceded by either an l or an h to indicate that the corresponding *arg* points to a long or short variable rather than an int variable.

e, f, or g cause a floating point number to be expected as the next input. The corresponding *arg* should be a pointer to a floating point variable. The input format of a floating point number may be a string of digits with an optional sign. The string may contain a decimal point followed by an optional exponent field. The exponent field may consist of an e or E, followed by an integer with an optional sign. The e, f, or g specifier may be capitalized. It also may be preceded by an l to indicate that *arg* points to a double rather than a float variable.

o causes an octal integer to be expected as the next input. The corresponding *arg* should be an integer pointer. The o specifier may be capitalized. It also may be preceded by either an l or an h to indicate that arg points to a long or short variable rather than an int variable.

s causes a character string to be expected as the next input. The corresponding *arg* should be a character pointer to an array of characters that is large enough to hold the string and a terminating \0 that will automatically be added to the string. The input field is terminated by a newline or space character.

u causes an unsigned decimal integer to be expected as the next input. The corresponding *arg* should be an unsigned integer pointer. The u specifier may be capitalized. It also may be preceded by either an l or an h to indicate that *arg* points to a long or short variable rather than an int variable.

x causes a hexadecimal integer to be expected as the next input. The corresponding *arg* should be an integer pointer. The d specifier may be capitalized. It also may be preceded by either an l or an h to indicate that *arg* points to a long or short variable rather than an int variable.

[causes string data to be expected as the next input. Leading white space is not skipped. The [is followed by a scanset (a set of characters which input characters must match). The scanset is followed by a]. At least one character must match in order for this conversion to be regarded as successful. The input field consists of the largest set of following characters that consists entirely of characters in the scanset. If a caret (^) appears as the first character in the scanset, it serves as a complement operator, redefining the scanset as the set of all characters not in the remainder of the scanset. The range of characters may be represented as *char1-charn*, e.g., [0123456789] can be [0-9]. The following conventions govern the scanset:

- The first character, *char1*, must be lexically less than *charn*, otherwise; the dash stands for itself.
- If the dash (-) is the first or last character in the scanset, it also stands for itself.

- If a right bracket (]) is to be included in the scanset, it must be the first character (perhaps preceded by a caret) of the scanset. Such a right bracket will not be interpreted as one of the brackets enclosing the scanset.

The *arg* corresponding to the left bracket ([) must point to a character array that is big enough to hold the string data field and the terminating \0 which is automatically added to the array.

Normal Completion: Value Returned

cscanf returns a count of the number of fields that were both converted and assigned. Fields which were read but not assigned are not included in the count.

Error Condition: Value Returned

cscanf returns EOF upon an attempt to read at an end-of-file. A return value of 0 means that no fields were assigned.

See Also

fscanf (Peterson 1992), scanf (Peterson 1992), sscanf (Peterson 1992)

dosexterr (DOS)	DOS SYSTEM CALLS	dosexterr (DOS)

Name

dosexterr—gets DOS error messages

Synopsis

```
#include <dos.h>

int dosexterr(buffer);
struct DOSERROR *buffer;
```

Description

dosexterr gets the register values returned by the MS-DOS system call 59H and stores them in the specified buffer. This function takes advantage of the extended error-handling facilities of MS-DOS Version 3.0 or later. Don't use the `dosexterr` function with MS-DOS versions earlier than 3.0.

Compile `dosexterr` with the `−dos` flag.

Arguments

buffer points to a structure of type DOSERROR in which `dosexterr` stores values returned by the MS-DOS system call 59H.

The DOSERROR structure is defined in the `dos.h` include file. It has the following form:

```
struct DOSERROR {
        int exterror;
        char class;
        char action;
        char locus;
        };
```

If *buffer* is a NULL pointer, `dosexterr` returns the value in AX without filling in the fields of the DOSERROR structure.

Normal Completion: Value Returned

`dosexterr` returns the value in the AX register. This value is the same as the value in the `exterror` structure field.

Error Condition: Value Returned

None.

See Also

`perror` (Peterson 1992)

eof (DOS)	FILE OPERATIONS	eof (DOS)

Name

`eof`—tests if end-of-file has been reached

Synopsis

```
#include <io.h>
```

```
int eof(handle);
int handle;
```

Description

eof tests whether the end-of-file has been reached for the specified file. Compile eof with the −dos flag.

Arguments

handle specifies the file handle of the file whose end-of-file condition is to be tested.

Normal Completion: Value Returned

eof returns 0 if the current file position is not end-of-file. It returns 1 if the current file position is end-of-file.

Error Condition: Value Returned

If handle is invalid, eof returns -1 and errno is set to the value of EBADF, indicating an invalid file handle.

See Also

ferror (Peterson 1992), perror (Peterson 1992)

| exit (DOS) | PROCESS CONTROL | exit (DOS) |

Name

exit—terminates the calling process

Synopsis

```
#include <process.h>

void exit(status);

void_exit(status);

int status;
```

Description

The `exit` and `_exit` functions terminate the calling process. `_exit` terminates the calling process without flushing any buffers. `exit` flushes all buffers and closes all open files before it terminates the calling process.

Compile these functions with the `-dos` flag.

Arguments

`status` receives a value that indicates a normal exit or an error condition. A value of 0 indicates a normal exit. Any other value indicates an error. After the calling process exits, `exit` or `_exit` makes the low-order byte of `status` available to the parent process, if one exists. The `status` value is lost if no parent process is waiting on the exiting process.

Normal Completion: Value Returned

No value is returned.

Error Condition: Value Returned

No error value is returned.

See Also

`spawnl` (DOS), `abort` (Peterson 1992), `exec` (Peterson 1992)

---

fclose (DOS)   STREAMS OPERATIONS   fclose (DOS)

Name

`fclose`, `fcloseall`—closes streams except standard streams

Synopsis

```
#include <stdio.h>

int fclose(stream);
FILE *stream;

int fcloseall();
```

Description

fclose closes the specified stream.

fcloseall closes every open stream except stdin, stdout, stderr, stdaux, and stdprn. Each buffer associated with a stream that is being closed is flushed before the stream is closed. Also, each system-allocated buffer associated with a stream is released when a stream is closed, except that buffers assigned using setbuf are not automatically closed.

Compile these calls with the −dos flag.

Arguments

stream specifies the stream to be closed by fclose.

Normal Completion: Value Returned

fclose returns 0 to indicate that the specified stream was successfully closed.

fcloseall returns a count of the total number of streams closed.

Error Condition: Value Returned

Both fclose and fcloseall return EOF to indicate an error.

See Also

close (Peterson 1992), fclose (Peterson 1992), fopen (Peterson 1992)

fgetc DOS)	STREAM INPUT	fgetc (DOS)

Name

fgetc, fgetchar—gets a character from a stream

Synopsis

```
#include <stdio.h>

int fgetc(stream);
FILE *stream;

int fgetchar();
```

Description

fgetc reads a character from the specified stream, at the current file position, and increments the file pointer (if one exists) to point to the next character.

fgetchar reads only from stdin, the standard input stream.

fgetc and fgetchar are identical to getc and getchar, respectively, except that fgetc and fgetchar are functions, not macros.

Compile fgetc and fgetchar with the −dos flag.

Arguments

stream specifies the stream from which fgetc reads a single character.

Normal Completion: Value Returned

fgetc returns the character read.
fgetchar returns the character read.

Error Condition: Value Returned

A return value of EOF may indicate either an end-of-file or an error. Also, an EOF is a permissible integer value. Thus feof or ferror should be used to determine whether an error or end-of-file condition occurred.

See Also

fputchar (DOS), putc (DOS), getc (Peterson 1992)

| **filelength (DOS)** | **FILE OPERATIONS** | **filelength (DOS)** |

Name

filelength—gets the file length

Synopsis

```
#include <io.h>

long filelength(handle);
int handle;
```

Description

filelength returns a count of the number of bytes in a file associated with a specified file handle.

Compile filelength with the −dos flag.

Arguments

handle specifies the file handle of the file whose length is to be reported.

Normal Completion: Value Returned

filelength returns a count of the number of bytes in the file.

Error Condition: Value Returned

If *handle* is an invalid file handle, filelength returns − 1L, and sets errno to EBADF, indicating an invalid file handle.

See Also

chsize (Peterson 1992), ferror (Peterson 1992), stat (Peterson 1992)

---

flushall (DOS)   **BUFFER OUTPUT**   **flushall (DOS)**

Name

flushall — flushes every output buffer

Synopsis

```
#include <stdio.h>

int flushall();
```

Description

flushall writes the contents of all buffers associated with open output streams to the associated files. All streams stay open after flushall is called.

Any buffers that are full are automatically flushed without flushall being called. Buffers also are automatically flushed when streams are closed or when a program terminates normally without first closing its streams.

Compile flushall with the −dos flag.

Arguments

None

Normal Completion: Value Returned

flushall returns a count of the number of open input and output streams.

Error Condition: Value Returned

flushall has no error return.

See Also

fclose (Peterson 1992)

FP__OFF (DOS)   GET ADDRESS REGISTERS   FP__OFF (DOS)

Name

FP__OFF, FP_SEG—return the offset or segment of a pointer

Synopsis

```
#include <dos.h>

unsigned FP__OFF(longptr);

unsigned FP__SEG(longptr);

char far *longptr;
```

Description

The FP__OFF and FP_SEG macros return the offset and segment, respectively, of the specified pointer.
Compile the FP__OFF and FP__SEG macros with the −dos flag.

Arguments

longptr is the long pointer whose offset (FP__OFF) or segment (FP__SEG) is to be returned.

Normal Completion: Value Returned

FP__OFF returns an offset expressed as an unsigned integer value.
FP__SEG returns a segment expressed as an unsigned integer value.

See Also

segread (DOS)

---

fputc (DOS)	STREAM OUTPUT	fputc (DOS)

Name

fputc, fputchar — write a character to a *stream*

Synopsis

```
#include <stdio.h>

int fputc(c, stream);
int c;
FILE *stream;

int fputchar(c);
int c;
```

Description

The fputc and fputchar functions each write a given character to a specified stream (fputc) or to stdout, the standard output stream (fputchar). The fputchar function has the same effect as fputc(c, stdout).

fputc and fputchar are identical to putc and putchar, except that fputc and fputchar are functions, not macros.
Compile fputc and fputchar with the −dos flag.

Arguments

c is the character which is to be written to stdout by fputchar or to the specified stream by fputc.
stream specifies the stream to which c is to be written by fputc.

Normal Completion: Value Returned

fputc returns the character written.
fputchar returns the character written.

Error Condition: Value Returned

If either fputc or fputchar returns an EOF, ferror should be used to determine whether the EOF actually indicates an error condition, since EOF is a legitimate integer value.

See Also

fgetc (DOS), getc (Peterson 1992), putc (Peterson 1992)

| getch (DOS) | CONSOLE INPUT | getch (DOS) |

Name

getch—gets a character from the console

Synopsis

```
#include <conio.h>

int getch( );
```

Description

getch reads, and does not echo, a character from the console. No characters typed are echoed. The system executes an INT 23H (Control-C exit) instruction if a CONTROL-C is typed.
Compile getch with the −dos flag.

Arguments

None

Normal Completion: Value Returned

getch returns the character read.

Error Condition: Value Returned

No error value is returned.

See Also

cgets (DOS), getche (DOS), getchar (Peterson 1992)

getche (DOS)	CONSOLE INPUT	getche (DOS)

Name

getche — gets a character from the console and echoes it

Synopsis

```
#include <conio.h>

int getche();
```

Description

getche reads and echoes a character from the console. The system executes an INT 23H (Control-C exit) instruction if CONTROL-C is typed.
Compile getch with the -dos flag.

Arguments

None

Normal Completion: Value Returned

getche returns the character read.

Error Condition: Value Returned

No error value is returned.

See Also

cgets (DOS), getch (DOS)

inp (DOS)   CONSOLE INPUT   inp (DOS)

Name

inp—reads a byte from a specified port.

Synopsis

```
#include <conio.h>

int inp(port);
unsigned port;
```

Description

inp reads a byte from the specified input port.
Compile inp with the −dos flag.

Arguments

port specifies the input port from which a byte is to be read. *port* may
be any unsigned integer in the range from 0 through 65,535.

Normal Completion: Value Returned

inp returns the byte it reads from *port*.

Error Condition: Value Returned

No error value is returned.

See Also

outp (DOS)

int86 (DOS)   SOFTWARE INTERRUPTS   int86 (DOS)

Name

int86 — executes an 8086 software interrupt

Synopsis

```
#include <dos.h>

int int86(intrno, inpregs, outpregs);
```

```
int intrno;
union REGS *inpregs;
union REGS *outpregs;
```

Description

int86 executes the specified 8086 software interrupt; int86 is designed to invoke DOS interrupts directly.

Compile int86 with the −dos flag.

Arguments

inpregs specifies the union whose contents are to be copied into the 8086 registers before int86 executes the interrupt. The union is of type REGS, defined in the dos.h include file. inpregs does not include segment register values.

intrno specifies the 8086 software interrupt to be executed.

outpregs specifies the union which receives the current contents of the 8086 registers after the specified 8086 software interrupt returns. The union is of type REGS, defined in the dos.h include file. outpregs does not include segment register values.

Normal Completion: Value Returned

int86 returns the value that is in the AX register after the interrupt returns.

Error Condition: Value Returned

If the flag field in outpregs is not zero, an error has occurred. The doserrno variable is set to the error code corresponding to the error.

See Also

bdos (DOS), intdos (DOS), intdosx (DOS), int86x (DOS)

---

int86x (DOS)   SOFTWARE INTERRUPTS   int86x (DOS)

Name

int86x — executes an 8086 software interrupt

Synopsis

```
#include <dos.h>

int86x(intrno, inpregs, outpregs, segregs);
int intrno;
union REGS *inpregs;
union REGS *outpregs;
struct SREGS *segregs;
```

Description

int86x executes the specified interrupt (see the *intrno* argument below). Unlike int86, the int86x function uses segment register values (see the *segregs* argument below) so that programs can use long model data segments or far pointers. The int86x function restores the value of the DX register after the interrupt returns.

Compile int86x with the −dos flag.

Arguments

inpregs contains values to be copied to 8086 registers before the interrupt is executed. The *inpregs* argument is a union having type REGS, defined in the dos.h include file.

intrno specifies the 8086 software interrupt to be executed by int86x.

outpregs receives the current register values that int86x copies to it after the interrupt returns. The *outpregs* argument is a union having type REGS, defined in the dos.h include file.

cflag is a field of *outpregs* that contains the status of the system carry flag after the interrupt returns.

flag is a field of *outpregs* that, if it is non-zero, indicates an error has occurred.

segregs specifies segment register values which int86x copies to the corresponding segment registers before executing the interrupt. The segread function or the FPSEG macro can be used to get the values to be put in the *segregs* argument. Only the DS and ES values in *segregs* are used by int86x. The *segregs* argument is a structure of type SREGS, defined in the dos.h include file.

Normal Completion: Value Returned

int86x returns the value that is in the AX register after the interrupt returns.

Error Condition: Value Returned

If the *flag* field in *outregs* is not zero, an error has occurred. The doserrno variable is set to the error code corresponding to the error.

See Also

bdos (DOS), FP_SEG (DOS), intdos (DOS), intdosx (DOS), int86 (DOS), segread (DOS)

---

intdos (DOS)	DOS SYSTEM CALLS	intdos (DOS)

Name

intdos — invokes a DOS system call

Synopsis

```
#include <dos.h>

int intdos(inpregs, outpregs);
union REGS *inpregs;
union REGS *outpregs;
```

Description

intdos executes an INT 21H instruction, invoking the specified DOS system call. intdos is designed to invoke DOS system calls that take their arguments in registers other than DX (DH/DL), or to invoke system calls that report errors by setting the carry flag.

Compile intdos with the −dos flag.

Arguments

inpregs contains register values that specify the DOS system call to be executed by intdos. Before executing the system call, intdos copies the values in *inpregs* to the corresponding 8086 registers. The *inpregs* argument is a union of type REGS, defined in the dos.h include file.

outpregs receives the current register values that intdos copies to it after the INT instruction returns. The *outpregs* argument is a union of type REGS, defined in the dos.h include file.

cflag is a field of *outpregs* that receives the value of the system status flag, copied to it after INT returns.

flag is a field in *outpregs* that, if it is nonzero, indicates that an error has occurred.

Normal Completion: Value Returned

intdos returns the value that is in the AX register after completion of the system call.

Error Condition: Value Returned

If the flag field in *outpregs* is not zero, an error has occurred. The doserror variable is set to the error code corresponding to the error.

See Also

bdos (DOS), int86 (DOS), int86x (DOS), intdosx (DOS)

| intdosx (DOS) | DOS SYSTEM CALLS | intdosx (DOS) |

Name

intdosx — invokes a DOS system call

Synopsis

```
#include <dos.h>

int intdosx(inpregs, outpregs, segregs);
union REGS *inpregs;
union REGS *outpregs;
struct SREGS *segregs;
```

Description

intdosx executes an INT 21H instruction, invoking a specified DOS system call. intdosx is designed to invoke system calls that take an argument in the ES register or that take a value in the DS register that differs from that in the default data segment. The intdosx call restores DS after the system call returns.

Compile intdosx with the −dos flag.

Arguments

inpregs contains register values that specify the DOS system call to be executed. The *outpregs* argument is a union having type REGS, defined in the dos.h include file.

outpregs receives the current register values that intdosx copies to it after the INT instruction returns. The *outpregs* argument is a union having type REGS, defined in the dos.h include file.

cflag is a field of *outpregs* that contains the status of the system carry flag after the interrupt.

flag is a field of *outpregs* that, if it is nonzero, indicates that an error has occurred.

segregs specifies segment register values which intdosx copies to the corresponding segment registers before executing the DOS system call. The *segread* function or the FP_SEG macro can get values to be put in the *segregs* argument. Only the DS and ES values in *segregs* are used. The *segregs* argument is a structure of type SREGS, defined in the dos.h include file. The *segregs* argument lets programs that use far pointers or long model data segments determine which pointer or segment is to be used during the system call.

Normal Completion: Value Returned

intdosx returns the value that is in the AX register after completion of the system call.

Error Condition: Value Returned

If the *flag* field in *outregs* is not zero, an error has occurred. The doserrno variable is set to the error code corresponding to the error.

See Also

bdos (DOS), FP_SEG (DOS), intdos (DOS), segread (DOS)

---

isatty (DOS)   **FILE OPERATIONS**   **isatty (DOS)**

Name

isatty—tests if *handle* is associated with a character device.

Synopsis

```
#include <io.h>

int isatty(handle);
int handle;
```

Description

isatty tests whether or not the specified file handle is associated with a character device: a console, printer, serial port, or terminal.
Compile isatty with the —dos flag.

Arguments

handle specifies a file handle to be tested.

Normal Completion: Value Returned

If the device is a character device, isatty returns a nonzero value. Otherwise, it returns zero.

Error Condition: Value Returned

None.

itoa (DOS)	VARIABLE CONVERSION	itoa (DOS)

Name

itoa—converts integers to a character string

Synopsis

```
#include <stdlib.h>

char *itoa(nvalue, string, radix);
int nvalue;
char *string;
int radix;
```

Description

itoa converts digits of a specified value to a null-terminated character string and stores the string.
Compile itoa with the —dos flag.

Arguments

nvalue is an integer to be converted to a character string.

radix specifies the base of *nvalue*. It must be in the range from 2 to 36. If *radix* is 10 and *nvalue* is negative, the first character of the stored *string* is a minus sign ($-$).

string receives the results of the conversion from a numeric value to a null-terminated character string. The space allocated for *string* must be large enough to contain the number of bytes expected in the return string. Up to 17 bytes may be returned.

Normal Completion: Value Returned

itoa returns a pointer to the specified string.

Error Condition: Value Returned

None.

See Also

ltoa (DOS), ultoa (DOS)

kbhit (DOS)	CONSOLE INPUT	kbhit (DOS)

Name

kbhit—checks the console for a keystroke

Synopsis

```
#include <conio.h>

int kbhit();
```

Description

kbhit tests for a recent console keystroke.
Compile kbhit with the −dos flag.

Arguments

None

Normal Completion: Value Returned

kbhit returns a nonzero value if any key has been pressed; otherwise, it returns zero.

Error Condition: Value Returned

None

labs (DOS)	**INTEGER OPERATIONS**	**labs (DOS)**

Name

labs — returns the absolute value of a long integer

Synopsis

```
#include <stdlib>

long labs(n);
long n;
```

Description

labs returns the absolute value of its long integer argument. Compile labs with the −dos flag.

Arguments

n is a long integer whose absolute value is to be found.

Normal Completion: Value Returned

labs returns the absolute value of n, its argument.

Error Condition: Value Returned

None.

See Also

abs (Peterson 1992), fabs (Peterson 1992), hypot (Peterson 1992)

Name

ltoa—converts a long integer to a character string

Synopsis

```
#include <stdlib.h>

char *ltoa(nvalue, string, radix);
long nvalue;
char *string;
int radix;
```

Description

ltoa converts the digits of the specified value to a null-terminated character string. It stores the result in a string.

Compile ltoa with the −dos flag.

Arguments

nvalue is a long integer to be converted.

radix specifies the base of nvalue. It must be in the range from 2 to 36. If radix is 10 and nvalue is negative, the first character of the stored string is a minus sign (−).

string receives the results of the conversion from a numeric value to a null-terminated character string. The space allocated for string must be big enough to contain the string returned; ltoa may return up to 33 bytes.

Normal Completion: Value Returned

ltoa returns a pointer to string.

Error Condition: Value Returned

None.

See Also

itoa (DOS), ultoa (DOS)

mkdir (DOS)   DIRECTORY OPERATIONS   mkdir (DOS)

Name

mkdir—creates a new directory

Synopsis

#include <direct.h>

int mkdir(*pathname*);
char *pathname*;

Description

mkdir creates a new directory having a specified *pathname*.
Compile makdir with the −dos flag.

Arguments

pathname specifies the pathname of the directory to be created. Since only
one directory may be created at a time, only the last component of the *pathname* can name a new directory.

Normal Completion: Value Returned

mkdir returns a value of 0 if it succeeds in creating a new directory.

Error Condition: Value Returned

mkdir returns a value of −1 if it fails to create a new directory. It also
sets errno to indicate one of the following error conditions:
EACCES means that the specified *pathname* is the name of an existing
device, file, or directory.
ENOENT means that the *pathname* was not found.

See Also

rmdir (DOS), chdir (Peterson 1992)

movedata (DOS) MOVE BYTES IN MEMORY movedata (DOS)

Name

movedata—copies bytes from a specified location

Synopsis

```
#include <memory.h>

void movedata(srceseg, srceoff, destseg, destoff,
numbytes);
int srceseg;
int srceoff;
int destseg;
int destoff;
unsigned numbytes;
```

Description

movedata copies a given number of bytes from a specified source address (expressed as segment:offset) to a specified destination address (also expressed as segment:offset). *movedata* is designed to move far data in small or medium model programs when the segment addresses of data are not implicitly known. Segment addresses in large model programs are implicitly known; this allows the use of the *memcpy* function.

movedata does not always handle overlapping moves correctly. However, *memcpy* always handles overlapping moves correctly. Overlapping moves are moves in which part of the memory area of the destination is the same as part of the memory area of the source.

Compile movedata with the −dos flag.

Arguments

destoff specifies the offset of the address to which bytes are to be copied.

destseg specifies the segment of the address to which bytes are to be copied. The appropriate *destseg* value can be gotten by using the segread function or the FP_SEG macro.

numbytes specifies the number of bytes to be copied.

srceoff specifies the offset of the address from which bytes are to be copied

srceseg specifies the segment of the address from which bytes are to be copied. The appropriate *srceseg* value can be gotten by using the segread function or the FP_SEG macro.

Normal Completion: Value Returned

No value is returned.

Error Condition: Value Returned

No error value is returned.

See Also

FP_OFF (DOS), segread (DOS), memory (Peterson 1992)

outp (DOS)	PORT OUTPUT	outp (DOS)

Name

outp—writes a byte to a specified port

Synopsis

```
#include <conio.h>

int outp(port, value);
unsigned port;
int value;
```

Description

outp writes the specified *value* to the specified output *port*.
Compile outp with the −dos flag.

Arguments

port specifies the output port to which the specified *value* is to be written; *port* may be an unsigned integer in the range from 0 through 65,535.

value specifies the value to be written to the port; *value* may range from 0 through 255 (1 byte).

Normal Completion: Value Returned

outp returns the specified *value*.

Error Condition: Value Returned

None.

See Also

inp (DOS)

| putch (DOS) | CONSOLE OUTPUT | putch (DOS) |

Name

putch—writes a character to the console

Synopsis

```
#include <conio.h>

void putch(c);
int c;
```

Description

putch writes the specified character, c, to the console.
Compile putch with the −dos flag.

Arguments

c specifies the character to be written to the console.

Normal Completion: Value Returned

No value is returned.

Error Condition: Value Returned

No value is returned.

See Also

cprintf (DOS), getch (DOS), getche (DOS)

| rename (DOS) | DIRECTORY OPERATIONS | rename (DOS) |

Name

rename—renames a specified file or directory

Synopsis

```
#include <io.h>

int rename(newname, oldname);
char *newname;
char *oldname;
```

Description

rename renames the specified file or directory from *oldname* to *new-name*. rename can move a file from one directory to another by specifying a different pathname in the *newname* (see below) argument. Directories can be renamed but not moved. Files cannot be moved from one device to another.

Compile rename with the −dos flag.

Arguments

newname specifies the new name to be given to the file or directory specified by *oldname*. *newname* may not specify the name of an existing file or directory.

oldname specifies the name of an existing file or directory whose name is to be changed. *oldname* must specify the name of a file or directory that already exists.

Normal Completion: Value Returned

rename returns 0 if it succeeds.

Error Condition: Value Returned

None.

See Also

creat (Peterson 1992), fopen (Peterson 1992), open (Peterson 1992)

rmdir (DOS)   DIRECTORY OPERATIONS   rmdir (DOS)

Name

rmdir—deletes a specified directory

Synopsis

```
#include <direct.h>

int rmdir(pathname);
char *pathname;
```

Description

rmdir deletes *pathname*, the specified directory.
Compile rmdir with the −dos flag.

Arguments

pathname specifies an empty directory which is to be deleted. The directory must not be in the root directory or the current working directory.

Normal Completion: Value Returned

rmdir returns 0 if it succeeds in removing the directory.

Error Condition: Value Returned

If rmdir fails to remove the directory, it returns −1 and sets errno to one of the following values:

EACCES means that the path specified by *pathname* is not a directory, or that the directory is the root directory or current working directory, or that the directory is not empty.

ENOENT means that the path specified by *pathname* was not found.

See Also

chdir (Peterson 1992), mkdir (DOS)

---

segread (DOS)   GET ADDRESS REGISTERS   segread (DOS)

Name

segread—gets segment register values

Synopsis

```
#include <dos.h>
```

```
void segread(segregs);
struct SREGS *segregs;
```

Description

segread copies the contents of the segment registers to a structure. seg-read is designed to be used with the intdos and intdosx functions to get segment register values.

Compile segread with the −dos flag.

Arguments

segregs points to a structure that receives the current contents of the segment registers, copied to it by segread. The structure is of type SREGS, defined in the dos.h include file.

Normal Completion: Value Returned

No value is returned.

Error Condition: Value Returned

No value is returned.

See Also

FP—SEG (DOS), intdosx (DOS), int86x (DOS)

| setmode (DOS) | FILE OPERATIONS | setmode (DOS) |

Name

setmode—sets the translation mode of a file.

Synopsis

```
#include <fcntl.h>

#include <io.h>
int setmode(handle, trmode);
int handle;
int trmode;
```

Description

setmode sets the translation mode of the specified file to the given *mode*. setmode is designed to modifiy the default translation mode of the stdin, stdout, stderr, stdaux, and stdprn files. However, it may be used with any file.

Compile setmode with the −dos flag.

Arguments

handle is a file handle that specifies the file whose translation mode is to be set.

trmode specifies the translation mode which the file is to have after set-mode executes. The translation mode may be one of the following:

O__BINARY sets the translation mode to untranslated node. This suppresses the translation caused by O__TEXT.

O__TEXT sets the translation mode to text mode. This mode causes carriage return/linefeed combinations (CR-LF) to be translated into single linefeed (LF) characters on input.

Normal Completion: Value Returned

If setmode succeeds, it returns the previous translation mode.

Error Condition: Value Returned

If setmode fails, it returns −1, and sets errno to indicate one of the following error conditions:

EBADF means that *handle* is an invalid file handle.

EINVAL means that the *mode* argument is invalid, being neither O__TEXT nor O__BINARY.

See Also

creat (Peterson 1992), fopen (Peterson 1992), open (Peterson 1992)

| sopen (DOS) | FILE OPERATIONS | sopen (DOS) |

Name

sopen—opens a file for shared I/O.

Synopsis

```
#include <fcntl.h>
#include <sys/types.h>
#include <sys/stat.h>
#include <share.h>
#include <io.h>

int sopen(pathname, fflag, shflag[,pmode]);
char *pathname;
int oflag;
int shflag;
int pmode;
```

Description

sopen opens the file specified by *pathname* and makes the file ready for subsequent shared reading or writing operations, as specified by *oflag* and *shflg* below.

sopen is meant to be used only with MS-DOS Versions 3.0 or later.

Do not use fdopen to associate a stream with a file opened for sharing or locking because file sharing modes do not work properly with buffered files.

Compile sopen with the −dos flag.

Arguments

oflag is an integer expression that is formed by combining one or more of the manifest constants shown in the list below. If more than one manifest constant is used, the constants are joined by using the OR operator (|). These constants are defined in the fcntl.h include file.

O_APPEND repositions the file pointer to the end-of-file position before each write operation.

O_BINARY opens the file in untranslated (binary) mode.

O_CREAT creates and opens a new file. If the file specified by *pathname* already exists, this has no effect.

O_EXCL returns an error value if the file specified by *pathname* already exists. This constant applies only if it is used with O_CREAT.

O_RDONLY opens a file only for reading. Neither O_RDWR nor O_WRONLY may be used if this constant is used.

O_RDWR opens a file for reading and writing. Neither O_RDONLY nor O_WRONLY may be used if this flag is used.

O_TEXT opens a file in translated (text) mode.

O—TRUNC opens and truncates an existing file to zero length; the contents of the existing file are destroyed. The file must have write permission.

O—WRONLY opens a file only for writing. Neither O—RDONLY nor O—RDWR may be used if this flag is used.

pathname specifies the file to be opened.

pmode specifies the permission settings of a file that is being created and opened for the first time, using O—CREAT. Otherwise, the *pmode* argument is ignored. Permission settings are set when the new file is closed for the first time. sopen applies the current file permission mask to *pmode* to determine how to set file permissions. The *umask* system service sets the file mode creation mask.

The *pmode* argument is an integer expression that contains one or both of the manifest constants S—IWRITE and S—IREAD. These constants are defined in the sys/stat.h include file. When both constants are present, they are joined using the OR operator (|). The meaning of each *pmode* argument is given in the following list:

S—IREAD means that reading is permitted.

S—IWRITE means that writing is permitted.

S—IWRITE | S—IREAD means that both reading and writing are permitted. The file is read-only if write permission is not specified. The modes S—IWRITE and S—IREAD | S—IWRITE are equivalent because, under MS-DOS, it is not possible to give write-only permission; all files are readable.

shflag is a constant expression that consists of one of the manifest constants in the following list. These constants are defined in the share.h include file.

SH—COMPAT sets the compatibility mode.

SH—DENYNONE allows read and write access to a file.

SH—DENYRD denies read access to a file.

SH—DENYRW denies read or write access to a file.

SH—DENYWR denies write access to a file.

The *shflag* argument is ignored by versions of MS-DOS earlier than 3.0.

Normal Completion: Value Returned

If sopen succeeds, it returns a file handle for the open file.

Error Condition: Value Returned

If sopen fails, it returns −1 and sets errno to indicate one of the following error conditions:

EACCES means that the sharing mode of the file does not permit the specified sharing operations, or that an attempt was made to open a file for writing but the file is read-only or the specified *pathname* is a directory.

EEXIST means that the __CREAT and __EXCL flags are specified, although the specified file already exists.

EINVAL means that SHARE.COM is not installed.

EMFILE means that no more file handles are available because there are too many open files.

ENOENT means that the specified file or pathname was not found.

See Also

close (Peterson 1992), creat (Peterson 1992), fopen (Peterson 1992), open (Peterson 1992), umask (Peterson 1992)

---

spawnl (DOS)   **PROCESS CONTROL**   **spawnl (DOS)**

Name

spawnl, spawnvp — creates and executes a new process.

Synopsis

```
#include <stdio.h>
#include <process.h>

int spawnl(modeflag, pathname, arg0, . . . argn,
NULL);

int spawnle(modeflag, pathname, arg0, . . . argn,
NULL, envp);

int spawnlp(modeflag, pathname, arg0 . . . argn,
NULL);

int spawnv(modeflag, pathname, argv);

int spawnve(modeflag, pathname, argv, envp);

int spawnvp(modeflag, pathname, argv);

int modeflag;
char *pathname;
char *arg0 ... *argn;
char *argv[ ];
char *envp[ ];
```

Description

spawn creates and executes a new child process. There are six different spawn functions: spawnl, spawnle, spawnlp, spawnv, spawnve, and spawnvp. These functions differ in three ways:

- Two functions (spawnlp and spawnvp) search the directories specified by the PATH environment variable for the file to execute. The search procedure used by the other four functions (spawnl, spawnle, spawnv, and spawnve) is described in the "Arguments" section below, in the entry for the *pathname* argument of the spawnle function.
- Two of the functions (spawnle and spawnve) cause the child process to inherit the environment variable setting of the parent process. The other four functions (spawnl, spawnlp, spawnv, and spawnvp) can change the environment variables of the child process. See the description of the envp argument of spawnle below for details.
- Three of the functions (spawnl, spawnle, and spawnlp) accept a fixed number of arguments. See the descriptions of the *arg0* . . . *argn* and NULL arguments of the spawnl function below for details. Three of the functions (spawnv, spawnve, and spawnvp) accept a variable number of arguments. See the descriptions of the *argv* argument of the spawnv function below for details.

The combinations of conditions satisfied by the six functions are as follows:

spawnl
- There is a fixed number of arguments.
- The directories to be searched are specified by *pathname*.
- The child process inherits the environment of the parent process.

spawnle
- There is a fixed number of arguments.
- The directories to be searched are specified by *pathname*.
- spawnle can change the environment of the child process.

spawnlp
- There is a fixed number of arguments.
- The directories to be searched are specified by the PATH environment variable.
- The child process inherits the environment of the parent process.

spawnv
- There is a variable number of arguments.
- The directories to be searched are specified by *pathname*.
- The child process inherits the environment of the parent process.

spawnve
- There is a variable number of arguments.
- The directories to be searched are specified by *pathname.*
- spawnve can change the environment of the child process.

spawnvp
- There is a variable number of arguments.
- The directories to be searched are specified by the PATH environment variable.
- The child process inherits the environment of the parent process.

Files that remain open when a version of spawn is called remain open in the child process. However, the spawn calls do not save the translation mode of open files. If the child process needs to use files inherited from the parent process, the setmode routine must be used to set the translation mode of these files to the required mode.

Signal settings are not saved in child processes that are created by calls to spawn routines. Instead, the signal settings are reset to their default values in the child process.

Use the −dos flag in compiling these calls.

Arguments

The arguments of the six different spawn functions are listed separately below.

spawnl
arg0 . . . *argn* are pointers to character strings that form the argument list for the child process. Argument pointers are passed as separate arguments to spawnl, spawnle, or spawnlp. At least one argument, *arg0*, must be passed to the child process when spawnl, spawnle, or spawnlp is called. By convention, *arg0* is a copy of the pathname, but a different value will not produce an error. For versions of MS-DOS earlier than 3.0, the value of *arg0* is not available to the child process. For versions 3.0 or later, the *pathname* is available as *arg0*.

The total length of strings that form the argument list must be 128 bytes or less. The space characters that are automatically inserted to separate the arguments are included in the count of total bytes, but the terminating null character of each string (∖0) is not included.

modeflag determines the action taken by the parent process before and during the spawn. Values of *modeflag* are defined in the process.h include file. They are as follows:

P␣NOWAIT causes the parent process to continue to execute concurrently with the child process. The P_NOWAIT *modeflag* value is reserved for possible implementation. Its use now causes an error value to be returned. See the error conditions below.

P_OVERLAY overlays the parent process with the child process. This destroys the parent process, as an exec call does.

P_WAIT suspends the parent process until the child process has completed execution.

NULL is required, following *argn*, in order to mark the end of the argument list.

pathname specifies a file to be executed as the child process. The *pathname* can specify a filename, a path from the root (full path), or a path from the current working directory (partial path). If *pathname* has a file extension, that extension is used in searching for the file. If *pathname* ends in a period (.), spawn calls use no file extension in searching for the file. If a *pathname* does not end in a period (.) or have a file extension, spawn calls append the extension .COM before searching for a file. If the search is unsuccessful, spawn calls attempt a search with an .EXE extension.

spawnle

arg0 . . . *argn* has the same meaning as in spawnl above.

envp is used only with the spawnle and spawnve versions of spawn. These two versions of spawn use the *envp* argument to pass a list of environment settings that alter the environment of the child process. The *envp* argument is an array of character pointers. Each pointer element of the array points to a null-terminated string that defines an environment variable. The strings have the form

NAME = *value*

where NAME gives the name of an environment variable and *value* is the value to which the NAME variable is set; *value* is not enclosed in double quotes. If *envp* is NULL, the child process inherits the environment settings belonging to the parent process.

modeflag has the same meaning as in spawnl above.

NULL is required, following *argn*, in order to mark the end of the argument list.

pathname has the same meaning as in spawnl above.

spawnlp

arg0 ... *argn* has the same meaning as in spawnl above.

modeflag has the same meaning as in spawnl above.

NULL is required, following *argn*, in order to mark the end of the argument list.

pathname has the same meaning as in spawnl above. In addition, the spawnlp and spawnvp calls search for the file specified by *pathname* in the directories given in the PATH environment variable.

spawnv

argv is an array of pointers to the separate arguments of spawnv, spawnve, or spawnvp. At least one argument, *arg[0]*, must be passed to the child process when spawnv, spawnve, or spawnvp is called. *argv[n+1]* must be a NULL pointer that marks the end of the argument list. By convention, *arg[0]* is a copy of the *pathname*, but a different value of *arg[0]* will not produce an error. For versions of MS-DOS earlier than 3.0, the value of *arg[0]* is not available to the child process. For versions 3.0 or later, the *pathname* is available as *arg[0]*.

The total length of strings that form the argument list must be 128 bytes or less. The space characters that are automatically inserted to separate the arguments are included in the count of total bytes, but the terminating null character of each string ($\backslash$0) is not included.

modeflag has the same meaning as in spawnl above.

pathname has the same meaning as in spawnl above.

spawnve

argv has the same meaning as in spawnv above.

envp has the same meaning as in spawnle above.

modeflag has the same meaning as in spawnl above.

pathname has the same meaning as in spawnl above.

spawnvp

argv has the same meaning as in spawnv above.

modeflag has the same meaning as in spawnl above.

pathname has the same meaning as in spawnl above. In addition, the spawnlp and spawnvp calls search for the file specified by *pathname* in the directories given in the PATH environment variable.

Normal Completion: Value Returned

If spawn succeeds, it returns the exit status of the child process, which is 0 if the child process has terminated normally. If the child process calls the exit routine with a nonzero argument, the exit status is set to that value. If the exit status was not set to a positive value by the child process, a positive exit status indicates that the child process was terminated abnormally by an `abort` or interrupt.

Error Condition: Value Returned

If `spawn` fails (the child process is not started), `spawn` returns -1 and sets `errno` to indicate one of the following error conditions:

`E2BIG` means that the argument list is longer than 128 bytes or that the environment information requires a space larger than 32K bytes.

`EINVAL` means that the *modeflag* argument is invalid.

`ENOENT` means that the specified file or pathname was not found.

`ENOEXEC` means that the specified file has an invalid file format or is not executable.

`ENOMEM` means that there is not enough memory available to execute the child process.

See Also

`abort` (Peterson 1992), `exec` (Peterson 1992), `exit` (Peterson 1992)

strlen (DOS)	STRING OPERATIONS	strlen (DOS)

Name

`strlen` — returns the length of a character string

Synopsis

```
#include <string.h>

int strlen(string);
char *string;
```

Description

`strlen` returns a count of the length, in bytes, of the specified *string*. Compile `strlen` with the $-$`dos` flag.

Arguments

string specifies the character string whose length is to be returned by `strlen`.

Normal Completion: Value Returned

strlen returns a count of the number of bytes in *string*.

Error Condition: Value Returned

None.

strlwr (DOS)	STRING OPERATIONS	strlwr (DOS)

Name

strlwr — converts uppercase characters to lowercase

Synopsis

```
#include <string.h>

char *strlwr(string);
char *string;
```

Description

strlwr converts any uppercase characters in a specified null-terminated string to lowercase.
Compile strlwr with the −dos flag.

Arguments

string specifies the string containing uppercase characters to be converted to lowercase.

Normal Completion: Value Returned

strlwr returns a pointer to the *string* that holds the converted characters.

Error Condition: Value Returned

None.

See Also

strupr (DOS)

Name

strrev—reverses the order of characters in a string

Synopsis

```
#include <string.h>

char *strrev(string);
char *string;
```

Description

strrev reverses the order of characters in the specified string. It retains the terminating null character ($\backslash$0).
Compile strrev with the −dos flag.

Arguments

string specifies the string containing characters whose order is to be reversed.

Normal Completion: Value Returned

strrev returns a pointer to the changed string that holds characters in reverse order.

Error Condition: Value Returned

None.

See Also

strcat (Peterson 1992), strset (DOS)

Name

strset — sets all characters in a string to the same character

Synopsis

```
#include <string.h>

char *strset(string, c);
char *string;
char c;
```

Description

strset sets all characters of the specified string except the terminating null character ($\backslash$0) equal to the specified character, c.

Compile strset with the −dos flag.

Arguments

c is the character which is to fill each character position in *string*.

string specifies the string which is to have all of its characters set to c.

Normal Completion: Value Returned

strset returns a pointer to the *string* that holds the specified new character, c.

Error Condition: Value Returned

None.

See Also

string (Peterson 1992)

---

strupr (DOS)   **STRING OPERATIONS**   **strupr (DOS)**

Name

strupr — converts lowercase characters to uppercase

Synopsis

```
#include <string.h>
```

```
char *strupr(string);
char *string;
```

Description

strupr converts any lowercase characters in the specified string to upper-case.
Compile strupr with the −dos flag.

Arguments

string specifies the string containing lowercase characters to be converted to uppercase.

Normal Completion: Value Returned

strupr returns a pointer to the altered *string* that holds the uppercase character.

Error Condition: Value Returned

None.

See Also

strlwr (DOS)

tell (DOS)	FILE OPERATIONS	tell (DOS)

Name

tell—gets the current position of the file pointer

Synopsis

```
#include <io.h>

long tell(handle);
int handle;
```

Description

tell obtains the current position of the file pointer (if one exists) associated with a specified file handle.
Compile tell with the −dos flag.

Arguments

handle gives the file handle of the file whose file pointer position is to be determined.

Normal Completion: Value Returned

tell returns the current position of the file pointer, in bytes from the beginning of the file.

Error Condition: Value Returned

If tell fails, it returns − 1 and sets errno to EBADF to indicate that *handle* is an invalid file handle argument. No return value is defined if the device (for example, a terminal or printer) cannot seek.

See Also

fseek (Peterson 1992), lseek (Peterson 1992)

ultoa (DOS)   VARIABLE CONVERSION   ultoa (DOS)

Name

ultoa — converts long integers to character strings

Synopsis

```
#include <stdlib.h>

char *ultoa(nvalue, string, radix);
unsigned long nvalue;
char *string;
int radix;
```

Description

ultoa converts the digits of a specified long integer value to a null-terminated character string.
Compile ultoa with the −dos flag.

Arguments

nvalue is a long integer to be converted to a null-terminated character string.

radix specifies the base of *nvalue*. It must be in the range from 2 to 36.

string receives the results of the conversion from long integer value to null-terminated character string. The space allocated for *string* must be sufficient to contain the returned string; ultoa can return up to 33 bytes.

Normal Completion: Value Returned

If ultoa succeeds, it returns a pointer to *string*.

Error Condition: Value Returned

None.

See Also

itoa (DOS), ltoa (DOS)

ungetch (DOS)	CONSOLE OUTPUT	ungetch (DOS)

Name

ungetch—pushes a character back to the console buffer

Synopsis

```
#include <conio.h>

int ungetch(c);
int c;
```

Description

ungetch pushes the character c back to the console buffer so that c can be read again by the next character read operation.

Compile ungetch with the −dos flag.

Arguments

c is the character to be pushed back to the console.

Normal Completion: Value Returned

If ungetch succeeds, it returns the character c.

Error Condition: Value Returned

ungetch will fail if it is called more than once before the next read. If it fails, it returns EOF.

See Also

cscanf (DOS), getch (DOS), getche (DOS)

BIBLIOGRAPHY

AT&T. 1990a. *UNIX System V Release 4 ANSI C Transition Guide*. Englewood Cliffs, NJ: Prentice-Hall, Inc.

———. 1990b. *UNIX System V Release 4 BSD XENIX Compatibility Guide*. Englewood Cliffs, NJ: Prentice-Hall, Inc.

———. 1990c. *UNIX System V Release 4 Device Driver Interface/Driver-Kernel Interface (DDI/DKI) Reference Manual*. Englewood Cliffs, NJ: Prentice-Hall, Inc.

———. 1990d. *UNIX System V Release 4 Migration Guide*. Englewood Cliffs, NJ: Prentice-Hall, Inc.

———. 1990e. *UNIX System V Release 4 Network User's and Programmer's Guide*. Englewood Cliffs, NJ: Prentice-Hall, Inc.

———. 1990f. *UNIX System V Release 4 Product Overview and Master Index*. Englewood Cliffs, NJ: Prentice-Hall, Inc.

———. 1990g. *UNIX System V Release 4 Programmer's Guide*. Englewood Cliffs, NJ: Prentice-Hall, Inc.

———. 1990h. *UNIX System V Release 4 Programmer's Guide: ANSI C and Programming Support Tools*. Englewood Cliffs, NJ: Prentice-Hall, Inc.

———. 1990i. *UNIX System V Release 4 Programmer's Guide: Character User Interface (FMLI and ETI)*. Englewood Cliffs, NJ: Prentice-Hall, Inc.

———. 1990j. *UNIX System V Release 4 Programmer's Guide: Networking Interfaces*. Englewood Cliffs, NJ: Prentice-Hall, Inc.

———. 1990k. *UNIX System V Release 4 Programmer's Guide: POSIX Conformance*. Englewood Cliffs, NJ: Prentice-Hall, Inc.

————. 1990l. *UNIX System V Release 4 Programmer's Guide: System Services and Application Packing Tools*. Englewood Cliffs, NJ: Prentice-Hall, Inc.

————. 1990m. *UNIX System V Release 4 Programmer's Reference Manual*. Englewood Cliffs, NJ: Prentice-Hall, Inc.

————. 1990n. *UNIX System V Release 4 System Administrator's Guide*. Englewood Cliffs, NJ: Prentice-Hall, Inc.

————. 1990o. *UNIX System V Release 4 System Administrator's Reference Manual*. Englewood Cliffs, NJ: Prentice-Hall, Inc.

————. 1990p. *UNIX System V Release 4 User's Guide*. Englewood Cliffs, NJ: Prentice-Hall, Inc.

————. 1990q. *UNIX System V Release 4 User's Reference Manual*. Englewood Cliffs, NJ: Prentice-Hall, Inc.

Christian, Kaare. 1989. *XENIX Command Reference Guide*. New York: John Wiley & Sons.

Hahn, Harley. 1986. *Mastering XENIX on the IBM PC AT*. Glenview, IL: Scott, Foresman & Co.

Kloes, David E. 1988. *The New Shell Game in UNIX & XENIX*. Houston, TX: Scribblers Publishing.

Microsoft. 1987. *Quick Reference Guide to XENIX Mail*. Redmond, WA: Microsoft Press.

Moore, Martin. 1986. *Working with XENIX System V*. Glenview, IL: Scott, Foresman & Company.

Peterson, Baird. 1992. *XENIX System V System Services: Programmer's Rapid Reference*. New York: Van Nostrand Reinhold & Co.

SCO. 1988a. *XENIX System V Development System: C Language Guide*. Santa Cruz, CA: The Santa Cruz Operation.

————. 1988b. *XENIX System V Development System: C Language Reference*. Santa Cruz, CA: The Santa Cruz Operation.

————. 1988c. *XENIX System V Development System: C Library Guide*. Santa Cruz, CA: The Santa Cruz Operation.

————. 1988d. *XENIX System V Development System: Device Driver Writer's Guide*. Santa Cruz, CA: The Santa Cruz Operation.

————. 1988e. *XENIX System V Development System: Macro Assembler User's Guide*. Santa Cruz, CA: The Santa Cruz Operation.

————. 1988f. *XENIX System V Development System: Programmer's Guide*. Santa Cruz, CA: The Santa Cruz Operation.

————. 1988g. *XENIX System V Development System: Programmer's Reference*. Santa Cruz, CA: The Santa Cruz Operation.

————. 1988h. *XENIX System V Operating System: System Administrator's Guide*. Santa Cruz, CA: The Santa Cruz Operation.

————. 1988i. *XENIX System V Operating System: User's Guide*. Santa Cruz, CA: The Santa Cruz Operation.

————. 1988j. *XENIX System V Operating System: User's Reference*. Santa Cruz, CA: The Santa Cruz Operation.

―――. 1988k. *XENIX System V Operating System: XENIX Tutorial*. Santa Cruz, CA: The Santa Cruz Operation.

―――. 1989a. *XENIX System V Development System: CGI Programmer's Guide*. Santa Cruz, CA: The Santa Cruz Operation.

―――. 1989b. *XENIX System V Development System: Device Driver Supplement*. Santa Cruz, CA: The Santa Cruz Operation.

SSC, Inc. 1987. *UNIX-XENIX Text Processing Reference*. Seattle, WA: Specialized System Consultants, Inc.

―――. 1989a. *Pocket Knowledge Pack: For XENIX V*. Seattle, WA: Specialized System Consultants, Inc.

―――. 1989b. *XENIX Command Summary: Version 5.2.3.2*. Seattle, WA: Specialized System Consultants, Inc.

Shaw, Myril C. 1986. *UNIX V & XENIX System V: Programmer's Tool Kit*. Blue Ridge Summit, PA: TAB Books, Inc.

Thomas, Rebecca. 1984. *The Business Guide to the XENIX System*. Reading, MA: Addison-Wesley Publishing Co.

Topham, Douglas W. 1989. *System V Guide to Unix and Xenix*. New York: Springer-Verlag, Inc.

Topham, Douglas W., and Trong, H. 1985. *UNIX and XENIX: A Step by Step Approach for Micros*. New York: Brady Books.

―――. 1986. *The System V Guide: A UNIX and XENIX Tutorial*. New York: Brady Books.

Waite Group. 1986. *Inside XENIX*. Carmel, IN: Howard W. Sams & Co.

Weber Systems, Inc. 1984. *XENIX User's Handbook*. Chesterland, OH: Weber Systems, Inc.

Woodcock, JoAnne. 1986. *XENIX at Work*. Redmond, WA: Microsoft Press.

INDEX

DOS cross development 117–172
  address register values 118, 155–156
  bytes, move in memory 120, 150–152
  cross development services
  directory, create 119, 150
  directory, delete 119, 154–155
  directory operations 119
  directory, rename 119, 153–154
  DOS cross development service description
    arguments 118
    description 118
    error condition: value returned 118
    name 117
    normal completion: value returned 118
    see also 118
    synopsis 118
    system call classification 118–121
  DOS error message 119, 129–130
  DOS system call 119, 121–122, 143–145
  DOS system call, invoke 119, 121–122,
    143–145
  file
    file handle, test 119, 145–146
    file length, get 119, 134–135
    file, open 119, 157–160

    file pointer 119, 169–170
    file, rename 119, 153
    file translation mode 119, 156–157
    shared I/O 119, 157–160
    test end-of-file 119, 130–131
  INT 21H instruction 121, 143, 144
  INT 23H instruction 139
  long pointer, offset of 118, 136–137
  long pointer, segment of 119, 136–137
  MS-DOS system call 59H 129
  Input
    console 119, 122–123, 126–129, 138,
      139, 147
    conversion character 127–129
    format 127–129
    format control 119, 126
    get character (console) 119, 138–139
    get character (console) and echo 119,
      139
    get character (`stdin`) 119, 133
    get character (stream) 119, 133–134
    get data 119, 126–129
    get string 119, 122
    keystroke, test for 119, 147–148
    read byte (port) 119, 140

integers
  absolute value of integer 120, 148
  convert integer to character 120, 146–147
  convert long integer to character 120,
      149, 170–171
interrupt, software 120, 140–143
Output
  console 120, 123–126
  conversion specification 123–125
  flush buffer 120, 135–136
  format 123–125
  print character (console) 120, 123–126
  push character (buffer) 120, 171–172
  put character (`stdout`) 120, 137–138
  put character (stream) 120, 137–138
  put string (console) 120, 126
  write byte (port) 120, 152–153
  write character (console) 120, 153
process control 120
  process, create and execute 120, 160–165
  process, terminate 120, 131–132
segment register 119, 155
streams 119
stream, close 119, 132–133
strings 120–121
  convert lowercase to uppercase 120, 168–
      169
  convert uppercase to lowercase 120, 166
  set string to same character 121, 167–168
  string length 120, 165–166
  reverse character order 120, 167

XENIX commands 3–116
  addresses 96
  alphabetic command list
    adb 7–16
    admin 16–20
    ar 20–21
    asx 22–23
    cb 23–24
    cc 24–32
    cdc 32–43
    cflow 34–35
    comb 36–37
    cpp 37–40
    cref 40–41
    ctags 41–42
    cxref 42–43
    delta 43–46
    dosld 46–47

    get 47–53
    gets 53
    hdr 53–55
    help 55–56
    ld 56–58
    lex 58–61
    lint 61–64
    lorder 64–65
    m4 65–69
    make 69–77
    masm 77–79
    mkstr 79–81
    nm 81–82
    prof 82–84
    prs 84–87
    ranlib 87–88
    ratfor 88–90
    rmdel 90–92
    sact 92–93
    sccsdiff 93–94
    sdb 94–101
    size 101–102
    spline 102–103
    strings 103–104
    strip 104–105
    tic 105–106
    time 106
    tsort 107
    unget 107–108
    val 108–110
    what 110–111
    xref 111–112
    xstr 112–114
    yacc 114–116
ANSI 31
archive table of contents 87
ASCII strings, find 6, 103–104
assembler, XENIX 8086/186/286 5
assembler, 8086/80286/80386 77–79
assembly 5, 22–23, 77–79
breakpoint 94, 97, 98
  C cross-reference table 5, 42–43
  C flowgraph 5, 34–35
  C language (also see compile)
  C preprocessor 5, 37–40, 62
  C program beautifier 5, 23
  C programming utilities 5
  C string extraction 112–113
  C string manipulation 5, 79–81, 112–
      113

compile
  C compiler 5, 24–32
  C compiler, XENIX 5, 24–32
  compile regular expression 5, 90
  compilation 5
  terminal information file, compile 7
compiler-compiler 6, 114–116
  accept action 114–115
  context-free grammar 114
  error action 114–115
  look-ahead token 114
  parser 114
  parsing operation 114
  reduce action 114–115
  shift action 114–115
  shift-reduce conflict 115
  reduce-reduce conflict 115
constant width italic type 1
constant width roman type 1
cross development utility 5, 46
cross linker 5, 46
cross-reference information 77–78
cross-reference listing 5, 40, 111–112
debug
  C debugging 34–35, 61–64
  debugger 5
  debugging 7
  debugging aids 5, 23–24, 40–43, 94–101,
    111–112
  symbolic debugger 94–101
  symbolic debugger commands 96–101
debugger, `adb` 7
  `adb` addresses 13
  `adb` expressions 14
  `adb` variables 12
  breakpoint deletion 11
  dot operations 8
  execution after breakpoint stop 11
  exit `adb` 8
  find matching words 8
  formatting 9
  inputting 9
  memory segment, create or modify 9
  outputting 9
  process termination 12
  program execution 11
  register names 13
  set break point 12
  subprocess management 11
  write to memory 12

disassembly 5
double-suffix rules 75
environment variable 71
execution time 6, 83, 106
external symbols 28, 83
file (*also see* SCCS *and* terminal))
  `a.out` file 56
  archive files 6, 20–21, 87–88
  COFF files 7, 20, 81
  common object file, absolute 81
  common object file, relocatable 81
  core image 94
  bss section 102
  data section 102
  error message file 5, 79–81
  `lex` files 34
  makefile 69–70
  modification date 20
  object file line numbers 6
  object file manipulation 6, 56–58, 81–82,
    101–105
  object file section size 6, 101–102
  object file symbol table 6
  prerequisite file 69
  text section 102
  target file 69
  `vi` tags file 5, 41–42
  `yacc` files 34
  XENIX file parts, display 7, 53–55
    relocation, long form 54
    relocation, short form 54
  `x.out` files 7
format of command descriptions
  description 3
  files 3
  name 3
  options and arguments 3
  see also 3
  synopsis 3
  warning notes 3
FORTRAN
  FORTRAN 88
  RATFOR control constructs 88–89
  RATFOR, convert to FORTRAN 5, 88–
    90
  RATFOR syntax 88–89
function pointer 25
global procedure 34
graph of external references 34
group ID 19

inference rules 72
internal macro 71
interpolate smooth curve 102
lex text analysis
  definition section 59
  lexical analysis 6, 58–61, 114–116
  rules section 59–60
  syntactical analysis 6, 58–61, 114–
    116
  user subroutine section 60–61
library management 6, 20–21, 64–65, 87–
  88
link edit 6
link editor 20, 24, 56–58
link editor directive 56
linkable object modules 22
lint 5, 61–64
loader 20, 88
machine-language instructions 97
macroprocessor 6, 65–69
manifest define 30
map listing 27
mathematical utility 102
memory models 25, 29
  compact model 25–26
  huge model 25–26, 29
  impure-text small model 25
  large model 25–26, 29
  middle model 25–26, 29
  pure-text small model 25–26
  small model 25, 29
object code 24
object library 6
object library ordering relation 6, 64–65
phase errors 20
pointer 95
preprocessor 6, 65–69
preprocessor directives 37–39
procedure name 94
process environment 68
profile 6, 82–83, 106
profile data, display 82–83
program configuration 28
program stack 27
random libraries 6, 87–88
RATFOR (*see* FORTRAN)
regular expression 90
Ritchie assembler 22
SCCS (Source Code Control System) 6, 16–
  20

ASCII text, generate from SCCS file 6,
  47–53
branch flag 86
ceiling boundary 86
ceiling (highest release number) 17
checksum 19
comment text 19, 33, 44
compare file versions 6, 93–94
cutoff date 48
data keyword 84–86
delta, announce impending 6, 92–93
delta branch number 49, 85
delta commentary, change 6, 32–34
delta, delete 6, 90–92
delta, execute 6, 43–45
delta information 85
delta level number 49, 85
delta line statistics 85
delta, null 18
delta release number 49, 85
delta sequence number 48–49, 85
delta table 85
d-file 19, 51
flags section 86
floor boundary 86
floor (lowest release number) 18
g-file 19, 44, 47–53
help 6, 55–56
identification keyword 48, 50
identify SCCS file 110–11
joint editing 48
keyword 18
keyword validation string 86
leaf delta 91
l-file 51–52
module name 49, 86
MR (Modification Request) number 18–19,
33, 44
MR validation 86
MR validation program name 86
null delta flag 86
pattern search 7, 110–111
p-file 19, 51–52
print SCCS file 6, 84
q-file 19, 52
SCCS commands
  admin 16–20
  cdc 32–43
  comb 36–37
  delta 43–46

get 47–53
help 55–56
prs 84–87
rmdel 90–92
sact 92–93
sccsdiff 93–94
unget 107–108
val 108–110
what 110–111
SCCS error messages 55–56
SCCS filename 49
SCCS file, identify 7
SCCS file parameters, alter 6, 16–20
SCCS file, validate 7
SCCS files, create 6, 16–20
s-file 16, 18–19, 44, 47–53, 84–87
shell procedure 6
shell procedure to reconstruct SCCS files
    36–37
SID, default 17, 86
SID (SCCS Identification String) 45, 50,
    85
SOH ASCII character 44
transient lock file (see z-file) 16
trunk successor 50

type indicator 91
undo get 7, 107–108
validate SCCS file 108–110
x-file 19, 52
z-file 19–20, 51–52
single-suffix rules 74
smooth curve, interpolate 5
sorting 107
stack 95–96
stack probe 28
streams 68
string extraction 5
string input 7, 53
structure 95
suffixes 72–73
symbol table 6, 27, 54, 81–82
symbol table, strip 104
terminal (see compile)
    terminal description 105
    terminal information utilities 7, 105–106
topological sort 6, 107
totally ordered list 107
version control 6, 69–77
XENIX compatibility 53–55
XENIX random library generator 87–88